Collaboration: What Makes It Work

Second Edition

Paul W. Mattessich, Ph.D.
Marta Murray-Close, B.A.
Barbara R. Monsey, M.P.H.
Wilder Research Center

FIELDSTONE
ALLIANCE

SAINT PAUL
MINNESOTA

We thank The David and Lucile Packard Foundation and
the Amherst H. Wilder Foundation for support of this publication.

Fieldstone Alliance is committed to strengthening the performance of the nonprofit sector. Through the synergy of its consulting, training, publishing, and research and demonstration projects, Fieldstone Alliance provides solutions to issues facing nonprofits, funders, and the communities they serve. Fieldstone Alliance was formerly Wilder Publishing and Wilder Consulting departments of the Amherst H. Wilder Foundation. If you would like more information about Fieldstone Alliance and our services, please contact us at

800-274-6024
www.FieldstoneAlliance.org

Edited by Vincent Hyman
Designed by Rebecca Andrews

Manufactured in the United States of America
Fourth printing, May 2008

Library of Congress Cataloging-in-Publication Data

Mattessich, Paul W.
    Collaboration—what makes it work / Paul W. Mattessich, Marta Murray-Close, Barbara R. Monsey.— 2nd ed.
        p. cm.
    Includes bibliographical references.
    ISBN 13: 978-0-940069-32-9
    ISBN 10: 0-940069-32-6
    1. Cooperativeness. 2. Interorganizational relations. 3. Human services—Management. I. Murray-Close, Marta, 1977- II. Monsey, Barbara R. III. Amherst H. Wilder Foundation. IV. Title.
    HM716 .M39   2001
    302'.14—dc21   2001003262

This 2001 edition of *Collaboration: What Makes It Work*:

- Identifies a new factor that influences the success of collaboration: An appropriate pace of development.

- Draws on an additional pool of 281 research studies.

- Brings in more research evidence to validate the nineteen factors in the first edition.

- Provides updated examples of the factors, based on experience of organizations throughout the world during the 1990s.

- Offers an expanded bibliography and list of contacts.

In addition, it offers several tools not contained in the first edition:

- The Wilder Collaboration Factors Inventory, a tool for assessing how a collaboration is doing on the twenty factors that influence success, along with instructions on interpretation. (This is also available as a separate booklet for collaborations to use in self-assessment.)

- Examples of how organizations have used The Wilder Collaboration Factors Inventory, and details on the process of self-assessment by a group of four collaborating organizations, along with a description of how they discussed their ratings and what action they took as a result of using the inventory.

- A description of how others have used the first edition, to offer new ideas to readers of this edition.

About the Authors

PAUL W. MATTESSICH, Ph.D., is director of Wilder Research Center, which dedicates itself to improving the lives of individuals, families, and communities through applied research. Mattessich has assisted local, national, and international organizations with strategic planning, organizational improvement, and evaluation. During the year that this revised edition was completed, he spent ten months in Northern Ireland, where he learned from, and consulted with, organizations addressing youth development, community development, and the promotion of peace and acceptance of diversity among groups from divided communities. Mattessich has been involved in applied social research since 1973, and is the author or coauthor of more than two hundred publications and reports. He has also served on a variety of task forces in government and the nonprofit sectors. He received his Ph.D. in sociology from the University of Minnesota.

MARTA MURRAY-CLOSE, B.A., (coauthor of the second edition) is a research assistant at Wilder Research Center. She conducts literature reviews and maintains literature databases for Wilder Foundation research studies. She is fluent in English, Spanish, and French and assists the center with multilingual interviewing and international communications. Murray-Close holds a bachelor of art's degree in psychology from Smith College.

BARBARA R. MONSEY, M.P.H., (coauthor of the first edition) was a research associate at Wilder Research Center and now lives in Seattle, Washington, coordinating clinical research projects for the Center for Health Studies at Group Health Cooperative of Puget Sound. She has formal training in anthropology and a master's degree in public health education from the University of North Carolina.

Acknowledgments

Many colleagues have contributed to Wilder Research Center's analysis of collaboration research and the development of *Collaboration: What Makes It Work*. The David and Lucile Packard Foundation and the Amherst H. Wilder Foundation provided funding for this second edition. Support from these foundations enabled us to do an objective, thorough analysis of the research literature. The first edition, in which we developed our methodology and synthesized research through 1992, benefited from funding from the Wilder Foundation, The Saint Paul Foundation, the United Ways of both Saint Paul and Minneapolis, and The Minneapolis Foundation.

To Barb Monsey, a coauthor of the first edition, we owe a great debt. Her pioneering efforts refined both the scientific methodology and the practical logistics for doing research that requires many, many hours of searching for completed studies, reading them, assessing them, and ultimately extracting significant information from them. Vince Hyman of Fieldstone Alliance nurtured our work from beginning to end. Readers of this edition will benefit as a result of Vince's insistence on clarity, completeness, logic, and fidelity to high research standards, as well as his attention to detail and development of a format that makes this book all the more readable. His intellectually stimulating challenges to our work resulted in an improved final product. Carol Lukas offered numerous suggestions and pieces of advice during the writing of the second edition, providing a perspective grounded in years of experience with multi-organizational efforts.

Tom Kingston, the president of the Wilder Foundation, encouraged the writing of this second edition and has given Wilder Research Center many forms of support, along with the freedom to do high-quality applied social research that will benefit individuals, families, and communities. Others whom we appreciate for their encouragement, advice, and assistance during this ten-year effort include Audrey Anderson, Rebecca Andrews, Bryan Barry, Bruce Bobbitt, Sally Brown, Ben Bushee, Marilyn Conrad, Phil Cooper, Lucy Rose Fischer, Ginger Hope, Heather Johnson, Christine Jones, Sharon Kagan, Louise Miner, Dan Mueller, Dawn Mueller, Greg Owen, Frank Romero, Gary Stern, and Michael Winer.

In addition, a number of experts on collaboration (whose names appear in Appendix C) participated in lengthy interviews to provide us with leads and advice. Many other researchers sent us copies of their publications when we were unable to obtain them by other means.

To all of these individuals, we express our thanks!

Contents

Preface to the Second Edition

As the completion of this book draws near, one collaborating author sits in Belfast, Northern Ireland; the other sits in Saint Paul, Minnesota. Technology that facilitates easy and cheap international communication just barely existed in 1992, at the time of publication of the first edition of *Collaboration: What Makes It Work*. Now, technology enables coworkers to correspond and transfer files intercontinentally as easily as if they sat in offices just down a corridor from one another.

Research and practice in the field of collaboration during the years before the dawn of the twenty-first century did not progress at the same speed of development as computer technology and the Internet. However, the field of collaboration did make gains. These gains motivated us to update the first edition. We felt it was important to seek out and review the research studies of the past decade and to discover whether research continued to validate the collaborative success factors identified in 1992. Even more important, we wanted to see whether research provided evidence of any new factors.

Belfast, Northern Ireland, as a divided society, offers a stimulating context for thinking about, researching, and doing collaboration. Several groups in Northern Ireland found the first edition of *Collaboration: What Makes It Work* very useful for developing plans for sustaining collaborative partnerships. The ongoing conflict, sometimes very violent, that permeates all aspects of this society tests the ingredients for collaborative success under extreme conditions. One can observe whether "mutual understanding and trust," "open and frequent communication," "shared vision," and other collaborative success factors identified in this book can grow among organizations to a level adequate to serve as glue that will attach divided parts of this society and sustain joint work to reach important mutual goals.

The Wilder Foundation has had a long-standing interest in the process of partnering among service-delivery agencies. The first Wilder publication to promote collaboration appeared in 1915. This second edition of *Collaboration: What Makes It Work* is a current example of that interest.

Reaction to the first edition, published in 1992, taught us that researchers and practitioners in the field of collaboration found it a useful tool. They appreciated the emphasis of the work on developing a practical reference for decision making that built upon credible, research-based information.

This edition, like the original work, establishes important theoretical groundwork for successful collaborative practice, based on the results of research. It provides a working definition of collaboration and distinguishes between collaboration and other forms of partnership, such as cooperation and coordination. It also includes discussion of the nineteen factors previously identified as influencing collaborative success.

What's more, this edition builds upon the initial work in several ways:

- Our review of collaboration research from the past decade led to substantial confirmation of the original nineteen factors and provided new evidence of their importance.

- We have enhanced many of the factor descriptions with fresh research examples, and have compiled an up-to-date list of collaboration references.

- In addition, we have made a number of substantive changes to the content of the initial publication. Based on our most recent research review, we have revised the names and descriptions of several success factors, and have identified new implications and interpretations for others.

- The review also led to the identification of a new factor related to the evolution of collaborations, which we have termed "appropriate pace of development." Recognizing that collaborative arrangements are not static, the authors of several studies noted a shift in the issues faced by collaborative groups over time. These authors suggested that the needs of collaborative groups differ across their life spans, with significant implications for effective collaborative planning. The dynamic face of collaboration, already implicit in the descriptions of several other factors, is presented in this edition as a factor in its own right.

Finally, this edition includes two entirely new chapters. Chapter Four describes ways in which the first edition has been used to advance both research and practice in the field of collaboration. Chapter Five presents The Wilder Collaboration Factors Inventory, an assessment tool designed to help others analyze their own collaborative efforts in light of Wilder Research Center's findings.

Goals of This Book

1. To *review and summarize* the existing research literature on factors that influence the success of collaboration.

   For the first edition of this work, we identified all research related to collaboration, screened out studies that didn't meet criteria for validity and relevance to collaboration, and combined the remaining set of studies to identify factors that influence success.

For this edition, we applied our screening procedures to the research literature that has been produced on collaboration since the time that the first edition went to press. We again identified studies meeting criteria for validity and relevance, and examined them with attention to factors deemed important for successful collaboration. Then, we compared our current findings to those from the first edition in order to confirm or modify the original nineteen factors, and to identify any new factors emerging from the recent research.

2. To **report the results** of the research literature review so that people who want to initiate or enhance a collaborative effort can benefit from the experience of others.

3. To **make available practical tools** that bridge the gap between research and practice.

While this book is not a "how-to" manual for collaboration, the present edition includes two new chapters that, we hope, will help readers make use of our findings. In Chapter Four, we provide some concrete examples of ways in which researchers and practitioners have built upon our work. In Chapter Five, we present The Wilder Collaboration Factors Inventory, an instrument that collaborative groups can use to assess their standing on the factors that may promote or inhibit their success.

Methodology

The findings presented in this book incorporate the results of our initial and current literature reviews. Our first review and summary of research related to collaboration, conducted in 1992, had three major stages. First, we identified all the research we could find related to collaboration. We searched through computer-based bibliographies, contacted researchers interested in the topic, and tracked down bibliographic references in each document obtained. The scope of the search included the health, social science, education, and public affairs arenas. From 133 studies examined, we screened out studies that were general "how-to" manuals, did not meet our definition of collaboration, or failed to meet other research criteria. After the screening, eighteen studies remained.

Second, we carefully reviewed each of the eighteen valid and relevant studies and identified factors that the studies reported as influencing the success of collaboration.

Third, we blended together the findings from the studies. We determined, for example, whether two researchers were using the same words to describe different factors, or different words to describe the same factor. As a result, nineteen factors that influence the success of collaboration were identified.

After the research was completed, we presented the nineteen factors at a conference on collaboration in the Twin Cities in May 1992. Participants suggested interpretations and added to the implications section for each factor.

Our most recent review of collaboration research employed the same basic methodology. In the first stage of the project, we identified 281 studies related to collaboration and screened out those that did not meet criteria for validity and relevance. We then examined the remaining twenty-two studies for findings that confirmed, contradicted, or added to the information presented in the first edition of this work. This process led us to retain the original nineteen success factors and to identify one additional factor.

At a national conference of collaboration researchers and practitioners in October 2000, we reviewed the findings for the second edition of *Collaboration: What Makes It Work* and invited comments and suggestions for this edition. Conference participants welcomed the new factor: An appropriate pace of development. Their experience with collaborations had already shown them that a key to effective collaborative work is mixing the ingredients for success into the stewpot in the proper order and on the proper schedule.

The first edition was written by Paul Mattessich and Barbara Monsey; this new edition is by Paul Mattessich and Marta Murray-Close. A detailed description of our screening and research procedures appears in Appendix B.[1] We present Appendix B to fulfill our obligation as conscientious scientists to describe our methods. We certainly invite any interested persons to pick up these methods in a few years and produce the next major synthesis of collaboration research. If no other collaboration aficionado chooses to do so, we might delve into another update for the next decade of research—unless we find ourselves in some exciting part of the world having so much fun collaborating on interesting projects that we just want to do collaboration, not analyze it!

We hope our work assists in your joint efforts with other organizations, and we wish you the best!

Paul Mattessich
Marta Murray-Close

May 2001

---

[1] Wilder Research Center has now applied this type of method to analysis of literature in several domains, for example: collaboration (this book and the previous edition); prevention programming (Mueller and Higgins, 1988); productive aging (Fischer and Schaffer, 1992); community building (Mattessich and Monsey, 1997); and rural violence (Monsey et al., 1995). The process has also been applied to a series of research reviews describing what research shows to be effective related to elementary school curriculum, instruction, school environment, and school-linked services including: Mueller (1997); Loch et al. (1997); and Gozali-Lee (1999).

CHAPTER 1

Introduction

SPRINGFIELD saw a rise in youth problems. Many youth were not completing their education; some boys were turning to gang activities; and more single, young mothers entered the child protection and welfare system.

Leaders from the schools, nonprofit social service agencies, youth organizations, health agencies, and government met to discuss how to make an impact upon the problems. Many agencies already provided services to teens, but many youth were falling through the cracks in the system.

After months of negotiation and discussion, the group applied for and received funding from a local foundation for a collaborative, school-based program for high-risk teens. Agencies would provide services at school such as health care and social service support. Springfield now anticipates a higher graduation rate, less delinquent behavior, healthier teens, and fewer teen pregnancies.

The Park Heights neighborhood was plagued by housing decay, transience, absentee landlords, and a lack of employment opportunities. Neighborhood organizations came together with the schools, police, social service agencies, and a neighborhood redevelopment agency to discuss what improvements might be made. Through the process of learning about each other and the different problems in the neighborhood, these groups joined together to start the Park Heights Neighborhood Initiative. The group now plans to develop goals and objectives for jointly improving the neighborhood.

Collaboration—An Effective Way to Work

Collaboration among human service, government, and community organizations intensified during the last fifteen years of the twentieth century. Why?

First and foremost, organizations have made a commitment to address social issues in new ways. Collaboration offers communities a tool to help them improve themselves. Organizations can join together in creative ways to tackle issues that lie beyond the scope of any single organization—issues such as housing, poverty, crime, jobs, or education. Not only are these issues large in and of themselves, but also they often relate to one another and defy the attempts of single-focus, independent organizations to deal with them. Schools alone, for example, can't be the only institutions to address education and youth development within poverty-stricken communities. And some national nonprofit organizations have achieved their goals by collaborating with small grassroots organizations that understand local needs and have an established reputation among the local population.[2]

Many community leaders and residents have hoped that collaboration will not only accomplish tasks that will improve community conditions, but also that collaboration will reinforce social fibers and increase the communities' capacity to get even more done. Collaboration depends on the existence of trust, shared vision, communication, and other ingredients. Fortunately, the process of collaborating *increases* the amount of these elements in a community. It builds stronger relationships that can then provide a foundation for more collaboration, addressing even more difficult issues.[3]

Chris Huxham, actively involved in collaboration research and practice on an international level for the past decade, sums up this belief in the efficacy of collaboration:

This rests on the belief that the really important problem issues facing society—poverty, conflict, crime and so on—cannot be tackled by any single organization acting alone. These issues have ramifications for so many aspects of society that they are inherently multi-organizational. Collaboration is thus essential if there is to be any hope of alleviating these problems.[4]

---

[2] The American Cancer Society, for example, remains each year among the twelve or so largest nonprofit organizations in the United States. Despite its size, the high quality of its work, and its esteemed reputation, it believes that it can only carry out its mission effectively if it develops collaborative partnerships with other organizations. So, it has pioneered a variety of approaches to promote collaboration with local, grassroots organizations to reach its public health goals. It also developed tool kits that, among other items, included materials from the first edition of *Collaboration: What Makes It Work*.

[3] Potapchuk and Crocker (1999) describe how the existence of what they call *civic capital* enables communities to develop collaborative strategies. As communities implement those strategies, their activities increase the amount of civic capital.

[4] See Huxham (1996 p. 4). A similar point is made by David Chrislip and Carl Larson in their 1994 book, *Collaborative Leadership: How Citizens and Civic Leaders Can Make a Difference*. Arguing that traditional leadership has failed to deal adequately with the challenges facing modern society, Chrislip and Larson call for a new era of collaborative engagement and civic community, in which organizations and individuals from different sectors work together to bring about societal change.

Changes in the ways communities must and do solve problems, coupled with changes in information technology may, in many situations, make collaboration the most effective tool for "bringing together a wide range of talents and resources to solve a problem, build a program, or create something entirely new."[5] As a result of significant changes in welfare legislation within the United States, many states developed, or encouraged the development of, collaborative networks within their borders to address welfare, poverty, and employment issues.[6]

Pressure from funders, beginning in the mid-to-late 1970s and continuing to the present, has also stimulated interest in collaboration. Formal mandates and government initiatives require many agencies to collaborate. Autonomy and "going it alone" are frowned upon in complex systems such as mental health, services for the handicapped, and youth employment.[7]

Economic realities have propelled organizations toward collaboration as well. A shrinking base of some traditional nonprofit resources has led many organizations to ask themselves if cost efficiencies could be possible by addressing common issues or delivering similar services together with their peers. Collaboration can reduce individual expenses in planning, research, training, and other activities. Throughout the life of a project, if overhead expenses are shared, duplication of cost and effort can often be avoided. (This is not to argue that collaboration always leads to cost savings. In fact, it may sometimes increase costs.)

Making services more accessible and effective is another potential benefit of collaboration. Helping people who have complex problems requires a great deal of coordination in order to provide the most efficient and effective assistance. Many organizations, in fact, now believe that the ability to get certain results can happen *only* through joint service efforts. Atelia Melaville and Martin J. Blank, researchers in the field of human service collaboration, emphasize that collaborative partnerships among human service agencies offer the ability to deliver services based on the *total* needs of clients—and the possibility of a truly integrated service system. A report, developed by The McKnight Foundation to describe its midpoint progress on an initiative to help families in poverty, stated:

Collaboration results in easier, faster and more coherent access to services and benefits and in greater effects on systems. Working together is not a substitute for adequate

---

[5] See Wilson (2000 p. 3).

[6] These states include New Hampshire, Illinois, Colorado, Washington, North Carolina, and others. See Sussman (2000) for examples and further references.

[7] See, for example: California A.B. 3015, Chapter 1229, Statutes of 1992, which established integrated systems of care as the model for children's mental health care in California; P.L. 99-660, The U.S. Comprehensive Mental Health Services Planning Act; P.L. 99-457, Part H, Early Intervention Program for Handicapped Infants and Toddlers; Title IV, Part A, of the Youth Employment and Demonstration Projects Act, 1977; National Institute of Mental Health and The Rehabilitation Services Administration agreement of 1978; Minnesota Comprehensive Children's Mental Health Act. The State of Ohio mandates the "clustering" of children's services, in order to promote at least a minimal level of collaboration among agencies serving the same geographic area.

funding, although the synergistic efforts of the collaborating partners often result in creative ways to overcome obstacles.[8]

In her highly regarded 1989 book, *Collaborating*, Barbara Gray notes that the quality of results often increases when a problem is addressed through interagency collaboration. This happens because organizations working jointly (rather than independently) are likely to do a broader, more comprehensive analysis of issues and opportunities. They also have complementary resources that "diversify" their capability to accomplish tasks.

Collaboration is not always effective. It is not always appropriate. Sometimes it might even result in greater costs than independent efforts. However, it does offer a strategic tool of value in many situations. Some people would predict that its popularity will continue to rise. Thus, understanding what makes it work becomes an important task to accomplish.

Addressing the Key Questions

What are the ingredients of successful collaboration? What makes the difference between success and failure in joint projects? What makes collaboration work?

Questions like these motivated Wilder Research Center's compilation of collaboration research. We've tried to answer them by taking information from case studies about collaboration and putting it together in a readable format. We reviewed a vast amount of research, extracted the major findings, summarized them, and drew a few critical conclusions. We hope the resulting publication offers important, accessible research material to anyone who wants to start a collaborative effort or better manage one in progress.

A Working Definition

The term "collaboration" is used in many ways and has a variety of meanings to different people. Here's our working definition:

> **Collaboration** *is a mutually beneficial and well-defined relationship entered into by two or more organizations to achieve common goals.*
>
> *The relationship includes a commitment to mutual relationships and goals; a jointly developed structure and shared responsibility; mutual authority and accountability for success; and sharing of resources and rewards.*

---

[8] See The McKnight Foundation (1991 p. 21). Another foundation, the Annie E. Casey Foundation, has turned this principle into action by developing collaborative demonstration projects to address the needs of at-risk youth in four U.S. cities. See the Center for the Study of Social Policy (1991).

In this book, we use *collaboration* to refer to the dynamic relationship defined above. We use the term *collaborative group* to refer to the set of organizations that join together in collaboration. The individuals who represent collaborating organizations are referred to as *partners* or *members*.

A discussion of the working definition of collaboration appears in Appendix A.

A Theoretical Basis for Collaboration

Besides a definition, this book identifies and discusses twenty keys to success in collaboration. **What the book *doesn't* do is act as a guide to specific actions in your situation.**

Let's say this book focused on gardening—rather than collaboration. In that case we would inform you, as reader and prospective gardener, about the basics of growing a healthy, productive garden. For example, we'd talk about soil conditions, the length of the growing season, and how much sunlight and water is needed to grow various plants. We would not, however, offer detailed instructions on how to plan and tend your own garden.

You would have gained from our material a sound *theoretical* understanding of what gardens need in order to bear fruit, but you would still have to apply that theory in your own, real-world situation. That's what we hope this book on collaboration will be for you: a source that illuminates the principles behind success and therefore provides insight into your own specific challenges.

How to Use This Book

Perhaps you're a funding agency that's actively seeking proposals for collaborative efforts, and need to know more about the subject. Maybe you're currently involved in a collaboration, and want some research results to back your hunches. Or maybe you'd just like some background information—a little homework on collaborations before you jump into one with your organization.

We hope that many people—program managers and planners, funders, policy-makers, and decision-makers in organizations large and small—will find it useful to have information on a set of ingredients research says is key to collaborative success.

Here are some ways to put this book to work:

- For general understanding:

  Read the book to increase your knowledge of the success factors behind collaborative projects. You will then have a set of useful concepts in mind when you consider collaboration as an option for achieving goals.

- In specific situations:

  Turn to the book when you need to plan or make a decision about a collaborative project. The material in Chapters Two through Five can serve you in at least three ways:

  1. Use the set of success factors as a checklist, or complete the collaboration measure in Chapter Five, to determine if your group's plans include all necessary ingredients. If not, you can take steps to build in whatever the project lacks.

  2. Use the content of Chapter Three (implications, discussion, and examples) to expand your thinking about ways to help your collaborative project succeed, comparing your situation with others that might be similar.

  3. After you have a collaborative effort under way, return to the material in the book to ask, What should we be watching out for? Are there changes we need to make in midcourse?

Chapter Six discusses in greater detail ways you can use this book.

CHAPTER 2

The Twenty Success Factors

THIS CHAPTER gives an overview of twenty factors that influence the success of collaborations formed by nonprofit organizations,[9] government agencies, and other organizations. Much of the research suggests that these factors can apply to collaborative efforts that link business organizations with nonprofit organizations as well.

The factors are grouped into six categories:

1. Environment
2. Membership Characteristics
3. Process and Structure
4. Communication
5. Purpose
6. Resources

Each factor from the research is listed, under its category, with a brief description. (The methods used to identify these factors are detailed in Appendix B.)

Each factor has check marks assigned, indicating the number of studies that identified the factor as important to a collaboration's success.[10]

We wish to emphasize that the factors should not be judged *solely* by the number of check marks they tallied. More check marks for a factor mean only that a greater number of studies identified that factor—not that it has a more significant impact on success. Research on collaboration continues, and future studies may provide a better understanding of the true importance of each factor. The bottom line is: to ensure the effectiveness of your collaborative effort, pay attention to *all* the factors listed.

For more detail on each of the twenty factors, please see Chapter Three.

---

[9] Outside the United States, among English speakers, nonprofit organizations would usually be called "non-governmental organizations," or among Francophones, *"organisations sans but lucratif."*

[10] "Number of studies" is used to show relative importance (rather than a more quantitative measurement) because studies of collaboration are almost all case studies, with nonquantifiable data.

Factors Influencing the Success of Collaboration

1. Factors Related to the ENVIRONMENT

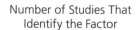

A. History of collaboration or cooperation in the community

A history of collaboration or cooperation exists in the community and offers the potential collaborative partners an understanding of the roles and expectations required in collaboration and enables them to trust the process.

✓✓✓

B. Collaborative group seen as a legitimate leader in the community

The collaborative group (and, by implication, the agencies in the group) is perceived within the community as reliable and competent—at least related to the goals and activities it intends to accomplish.

✓✓✓✓✓

C. Favorable political and social climate

Political leaders, opinion-makers, persons who control resources, and the general public support (or at least do not oppose) the mission of the collaborative group.

2. Factors Related to MEMBERSHIP CHARACTERISTICS

A. Mutual respect, understanding, and trust

Members of the collaborative group share an understanding and respect for each other and their respective organizations: how they operate, their cultural norms and values, their limitations, and their expectations.

B. Appropriate cross section of members

To the extent that they are needed, the collaborative group includes representatives from each segment of the community who will be affected by its activities.

✓✓✓✓✓✓✓✓✓✓✓✓

C. Members see collaboration as in their self-interest

Collaborating partners believe that they will benefit from their involvement in the collaboration and that the advantages of membership will offset costs such as loss of autonomy and turf.

D. Ability to compromise

Collaborating partners are able to compromise, since the many decisions within a collaborative effort cannot possibly fit the preferences of every member perfectly.

3. Factors Related to PROCESS AND STRUCTURE

A. Members share a stake in both process and outcome

✓✓✓✓✓✓✓

Members of a collaborative group feel "ownership" of both the way the group works and the results or products of its work.

B. Multiple layers of participation

✓✓✓✓✓✓✓✓✓✓✓✓
✓✓

Every level (upper management, middle management, operations) within each partner organization has at least some representation and ongoing involvement in the collaborative initiative.

C. Flexibility

✓✓✓✓✓✓✓✓

The collaborative group remains open to varied ways of organizing itself and accomplishing its work.

D. Development of clear roles and policy guidelines

✓✓✓✓✓✓✓✓✓✓✓✓

The collaborating partners clearly understand their roles, rights, and responsibilities, and they understand how to carry out those responsibilities.

E. Adaptability

✓✓✓✓✓✓

The collaborative group has the ability to sustain itself in the midst of major changes, even if it needs to change some major goals, members, etc., in order to deal with changing conditions.

F. Appropriate pace of development

✓✓✓✓✓✓

The structure, resources, and activities of the collaborative group change over time to meet the needs of the group without overwhelming its capacity, at each point throughout the initiative.[11]

4. Factors Related to COMMUNICATION

A. Open and frequent communication

✓✓✓✓✓✓✓✓✓✓✓✓

Collaborative group members interact often, update one another, discuss issues openly, and convey all necessary information to one another and to people outside the group.

B. Established informal relationships and communication links

✓✓✓✓✓✓✓✓

In addition to formal channels of communication, members establish personal connections—producing a better, more informed, and cohesive group working on a common project.

---

[11] This factor is new to the 2001 edition.

5. Factors Related to PURPOSE

✓✓✓✓✓✓✓✓

A. Concrete, attainable goals and objectives

Goals and objectives of the collaborative group are clear to all partners, and can realistically be attained.

✓✓✓✓✓✓✓✓✓✓✓✓

B. Shared vision

Collaborating partners have the same vision, with clearly agreed-upon mission, objectives, and strategy. The shared vision may exist at the outset of collaboration, or the partners may develop a vision as they work together.

✓✓✓

C. Unique purpose

The mission and goals, or approach, of the collaborative group differ, at least in part, from the mission and goals, or approach, of the member organizations.

6. Factors Related to RESOURCES

✓✓✓✓✓✓✓✓✓✓✓✓✓
✓✓✓✓

A. Sufficient funds, staff, materials, and time

The collaborative group has an adequate, consistent financial base, along with the staff and materials needed to support its operations. It allows sufficient time to achieve its goals and includes time to nurture the collaboration.

✓✓✓✓✓✓✓✓✓✓✓

B. Skilled leadership

The individual who provides leadership for the collaborative group has organizing and interpersonal skills, and carries out the role with fairness. Because of these characteristics (and others), the leader is granted respect or "legitimacy" by the collaborative partners.

CHAPTER 3

Understanding the Factors

THIS CHAPTER goes into more detail about each of the factors that influence the success of collaboration, as identified by the research literature.

Each entry includes

A **description**: one to three sentences explaining the factor.

Implications: a discussion of the factor's practical importance for those who wish to start or enhance a collaborative effort. These suggestions are based on our own analysis, using the observations of the original researchers as well as comments from readers of this book in its draft form and participants in a collaboration conference.

An **illustration**: at least one excerpt from a research case study.

1. Factors Related to the ENVIRONMENT

Environmental characteristics consist of the geographic location and social context within which a collaborative group exists. The group may be able to influence or affect these elements in some way, but it does not have control over them.

A. History of collaboration or cooperation in the community

Description

A history of collaboration or cooperation exists in the community and offers the potential collaborative partners an understanding of the roles and expectations required in collaboration and enables them to trust the process.[12]

Implications

- Other things being equal, collaborative efforts will most likely succeed where cooperative or collaborative activity has a history or is encouraged.

- When planning a collaborative effort, goals should be set according to the level of development, understanding, and acceptance of collaboration within the community.

- If a major, new collaborative approach seems worthwhile even though a community has little or no history of collaboration, environmental factors should be addressed before starting the work. Examples include advocacy for legislation and/or funding that promotes collaboration, as well as educating potential collaborators regarding the benefits and processes of collaboration.

- Some parts of a community may provide an inhospitable environment for collaboration. For example, organizations may have a history of competitiveness. When this is the case, or when a community has attempted collaboration and had a negative experience with it, more time may be required at the beginning of a collaborative initiative to build trust, common vocabulary, mutual expectations, and other success factors.

Illustration

A 1995 study of collaboration between agencies serving children with mental health problems notes the benefits of a history of positive experience with collaborations.[13]

The Division of Mental Health and the Department of Education were already collaborating formally and informally on a number of projects and this longstanding relationship was seen as an important factor in the successful collaboration among all four agencies within the auspices of AB 377 which also included Probation and Social Services. (Abbott et al., p. 306)

---

[12] Note two things. First, "community" can have a clear geographic base; but it can also refer to a set of people or organizations with common ties based on professional discipline, industry, ethnicity, or other affiliations. Second, the history of collaboration may not be of similar depth throughout a specific community. Organizations of certain types may have begun collaborative relationships long before organizations of other types.

[13] In each "Illustration" section in this chapter, case studies are referenced by the author's last name. Complete citations appear in the bibliography. In addition, Appendix D cross-references each study with each factor it identifies.

B. Collaborative group seen as a legitimate leader in the community

The collaborative group (and, by implication, the agencies in the group) is perceived within the community as reliable and competent—at least related to the goals and activities it intends to accomplish.

Description

- Collaborative groups that intend to make system-wide changes or work with the wider community must be perceived as suitable leaders by the communities they intend to influence.

Implications

- The early stage of a collaborative effort should include an assessment of the collaborative group's leadership image, and, if deficient, the collaborative group should correct this image.

- Community-wide projects require broad legitimacy. Smaller scale projects will require legitimacy in the eyes of a narrower group.

A 1991 study looks at a collaborative group in the garment industry that was applying for community development funds to start a job training program. The group found its poor reputation in the community posed a major barrier.

Illustration

In the past, the federal government's CETA program had regulations expressly precluding placement of workers in the sewing industry. The local economic development organizations believed that the "fly by night" reputation was deserved so, consistent with theory, they saw no reason to help the garment industry. A major effort in this collaboration involved persuading these funding institutions that the garment firms in this collaboration were dependable corporate citizens. (Sharfman et al., p. 24)

C. Favorable political and social climate

Political leaders, opinion-makers, persons who control resources, and the general public support (or at least do not oppose) the mission of the collaborative group.

Description

- Collaborating partners should spend time up front "selling" the collaboration to key leaders in order to create the best political climate possible.

Implications

- Often, the political and social climate acts as a positive external motivator to collaboration. For example, policy-makers may encourage collaborations as a way of tackling issues.

- If the right climate does not exist, collaborating partners should consider strategies and tactics for improving the climate—changing public opinion, for example, to achieve the collaboration's goals.

- Collaborative groups should set goals realistically to meet political and social requirements.

- A collaborative group's goals and the process undertaken to reach those goals should be perceived as cost-effective and not in conflict with (or a drain on) ongoing community endeavors.[14]

- The political and social climate can change throughout the life of a collaborative group. The climate should be monitored and action taken if it becomes negative.

Illustration   A 1997 study describes how members of a school-college collaboration used various strategies to develop a positive social and political climate.

Another element nurturing the collaboration has been the backing of parents, politicians, and community groups. We recognized from the start, both for reasons emanating from principle and from a desire to be effective, that there was a need to gain the involvement and support of other groups. In the beginning we worked with union representatives in the staffing of the school; we welcomed and encouraged the participation of parents; we joined with local groups and politicians to develop a school design that would serve the needs of the community. The effort to maintain the support of the various constituencies continues to this day. Proof of our effectiveness in this regard is evidenced by the fact that whenever there is even a whisper that the collaboration might be ended, parents, politicians, and community representatives rise up as one to resist the idea. (Trubowitz and Longo, p. 159)

2. Factors Related to MEMBERSHIP CHARACTERISTICS

Membership characteristics consist of skills, attitudes, and opinions of the individuals in a collaborative group, as well as the culture and capacity of the organizations that form collaborative groups.

A. Mutual respect, understanding, and trust

Description   Members of the collaborative group share an understanding and respect for each other and their respective organizations: how they operate, their cultural norms and values, their limitations, and their expectations.

Implications
- At the very beginning of an effort, collaborating partners should temporarily set aside the purpose of the collaboration and devote energy to learning about each other.

- Partners must present their intentions and agendas honestly and openly to bring out trust-building.

- Building strong relationships takes time. Collaborative groups should allow sufficient time for trust and understanding to develop.

---

[14] Neither of these last two implications is intended to imply that collaborative groups should always avoid actions that are politically controversial or that may lead to a revision in community priorities or funding patterns. Rather, they encourage strategic thinking on how to make collaborative efforts as productive as possible within a specific set of social, historical, and political circumstances.

- Time should be set aside to understand how language is used and how members perceive each other.

- Conflicts may develop due to a lack of understanding about the other partners in a collaborative group.

- Current connections through systems other than the proposed collaborative group provide a foundation for the communication, trust, and sharing that will be crucial to building a successful collaboration. If such connections do not exist, understanding why may be an important part of establishing the new group.

A 1997 study of collaboration among a school, several social services agencies, and the local police force and juvenile justice systems describes the process through which disparate public and private partners built a working culture of mutual trust and respect.

Illustrations

Along with the agreement at the executive level, a trusting relationship among the partners at the program level was critical to success. For all of the partners, trust was developed by participating in discussion and planning for overall program goals and individual child-family goals and by working together over an extended time. The process of developing trust and confidence in fellow team members began at program start-up. At that time, a committee consisting of representatives of the police department and the juvenile justice system, the school principal, and a parent of a child in the school interviewed finalists for the two case manager positions and made hiring decisions jointly. The process gave each institution a stake in the program and also served to bond individual team members to one another. (Tapper et al., p. 181)

A 1999 study of collaboration in the domestic violence field identifies mutual learning and open exchange as essential ingredients for building trust.

Mutual trust is required to reach consensus. Group members with different backgrounds and constituencies learn to trust each other as they communicate, learn each other's language, and work together to solve problems. Although a critical mass of prior connections and respect for each other's work formed a foundation for trust in the [Chicago Women's Health Risk Study], not everyone in the initial group was acquainted. However, reciprocal learning was evident from our first general meeting onward. Because every member believed in the importance of the research questions being addressed, they were willing to consider and evaluate others' points of view. Lengthy discussions at meetings helped group members listen to others' perspectives, develop shared values, and reach consensus. Each new resolution of a problem further enhanced mutual trust. (Block et al., p. 1166)

B. Appropriate cross section of members

Description
To the extent that they are needed, the collaborative group includes representatives from each segment of the community who will be affected by its activities.

Implications

- The group should carefully review who needs to be involved in the collaborative endeavor. It should take time to identify the people who have either explicit or unspoken control over relevant issues. These key people should be invited to become partners or to participate in the collaboration some other way.

- Partners should continuously monitor whether new groups or individuals should be brought into the ongoing process. A formal integration and education plan for new members should be developed.

- The cross section of members cannot be so broad and the number of collaborative members so great that the process of collaboration becomes unmanageable.

- If agencies are similar in terms of such characteristics as purpose, structure, areas served, or the kinds of clients served, they will already have some amount of understanding and interdependence upon which to build.

Illustration
A 1995 study examined the collaborative effort of public and private organizations to address New York City's youth unemployment problem. In her analysis of the case, the author points to the absence of key stakeholders as one of the reasons for the project's eventual collapse.

A final factor that thwarted implementation was the exclusion of some stakeholders from the Youth Policy Group. The YPG emerged out of the European trip and its members were largely those who had taken the trip. The stakeholder group that traveled together represented several organizations who had a real interest in the youth employment issue and historically were committed to improving the situation. However, other groups in New York who had a stake in the youth employment issue were not included. Groups who were not involved included the mayor's office, and youth and local groups in communities with high levels of unemployed youth. Their exclusion had the net effect of limiting enthusiasm for the project. These groups were in a position to create an interested audience and political support for the recommendations, but this never materialized. (Gray, p. 92)

C. Members see collaboration as in their self-interest

Description
Collaborating partners believe that they will benefit from their involvement in the collaboration and that the advantages of membership will offset costs such as loss of autonomy and turf.

- It should be very clear what member organizations stand to gain from the collaboration, and those expectations should be built into the goals so they remain visible throughout the life of the collaborative effort.

Implications

- Incentives for individual organizations to get involved and stay involved should be built into the collaborative effort, and those incentives should be monitored to see if they continue to motivate members.

A 1997 study explains how collaboration between a university and a community development corporation can serve the interest of both partners.

Illustration

The proposed development of a new family health clinic by TRP [the community development corporation] for UIC's [the university's] Medical Center is an example of creating collaborations that are mutually beneficial. The university had assisted TRP with an earlier community-initiated effort to reform the poor services provided at a public health clinic in Pilsen [the surrounding community], but despite repeated negotiations and proposals to the city, little progress was made. At the same time, the UIC Hospital was facing new competitive pressures as a result of health care reform. A movement toward managed care arrangements meant that the university would be at a disadvantage without more community-based clinics to create a large primary care patient population from which to draw tertiary care patients for its hospital. Medical center staff crafted a proposal to have TRP act as developers of a new community health center with UIC as the service provider. The project will enable TRP to leverage its expertise in real estate development to create a new facility that serves the needs of Pilsen, and UIC will have a new site in the community to position it to meet the competitive requirements of new managed-care programs. (Wiewel and Guerrero, p. 128)

D. Ability to compromise

Collaborating partners are able to compromise, since the many decisions within a collaborative effort cannot possibly fit the preferences of every member perfectly.

Description

- Participating organizations must give their representatives some latitude in working out agreements among partners. Rigid rules and expectations will render collaboration unworkable.

Implications

- Collaborative members should allow time to act deliberately and patiently when reaching decisions.

- Collaborative members must know when to seek compromise or common ground and how to amicably negotiate major decisions in situations where members do not initially share the same opinions.

Illustration   A 1999 study describes how one collaborative group reconciled the conflicting perspectives and priorities of a survey research center and a coalition of advocates for battered women.

When the collaboration began, there was no plan in place for reporting to the Governor's Commission on Domestic Violence. This could have put the advocacy agenda of the project leaders and the neutrality mandate of the researchers on a collision course because the research team members needed to be sure that the findings would be presented in a manner consistent with their roles as neutral fact finders, whereas advocates within the working group wanted the data in a form that would be most likely to influence policy. Instead of colliding or parting ways (another option for the group at this point), the various collaborators quickly agreed that the effort would produce two reports and that these would be offered to the Governor's Commission and the public as companion pieces. (Lennett and Colten, p. 1137)

3. Factors Related to PROCESS AND STRUCTURE

Process and structure refers to the management, decision-making, and operational systems of a collaborative effort.

A. Members share a stake in both process and outcome

Description   Members of a collaborative group feel "ownership" of both the way the group works and the results or products of its work.

Implications
- Adequate time and resources must be devoted to developing ownership among all participants in a collaborative effort.

- The operating principles and procedures of a collaborative group must promote among members a feeling of ownership about decisions and outcomes.

- Members' perceptions of ownership of a collaborative group need to be continuously monitored, and needed changes made in process or structure in order to ensure the feeling of ownership.

- Interagency work groups, participating in regular planning and monitoring of the collaborative effort, can solidify ownership and ongoing commitment.

Illustration   A 1995 study provides examples of how a lack of ownership and accountability on the part of the business community led to failure for a collaborative project.

The typical model of implementation within the New York City Partnership was the lead company approach, in which one corporate CEO spearheaded a project using his or her own staff resources to coordinate it. Since the Youth Policy Group plan did not operate with a lead company model, corporate support did not materialize. As one [collaborative member] explained, "No one

*could administer the joint agreement. The Partnership did not have the will
or the authority to do so." Ownership of the [collaborative group's] efforts
could have been more widely distributed had either or both committees ratified
the group's mission and formally charged it to return with recommendations.
Clarification about who was responsible for implementation would more likely
have occurred if there had been accountability to one of these committees.
Thus, the inability of the New York City Partnership to muster and sustain
high-level corporate support for the [collaborative group's] recommendations
was a major reason for the lack of implementation.* (Gray, p. 91)

B. Multiple layers of participation

Every level (upper management, middle management, operations) within each   **Description**
partner organization has at least some representation and ongoing involvement
in the collaborative initiative.

- Successful collaborative groups recognize the multiple layers of staff in   **Implications**
  each organization and create mechanisms to involve them.

- At the outset of collaboration, systems should be developed to include necessary staff from each organization.

- Linking leaders may not be sufficient to sustain a major collaboration. Inte-
  grating the efforts throughout all the members' systems builds stronger ties
  and increases the likelihood of success.

- It is important that talented, key people in an organization be assigned to
  work on the collaborative project and that they be interested in its success.

In a 1998 study of three university-community collaborations, the author dis-   **Illustration**
cusses the need to involve people from a variety of organizational positions in
the collaborative relationship.

*A reliance on connections among specific individuals should not detract from
the need to institutionalize the partnership. Faculty and staff at the university
and leaders of community organizations, foundations, and local governments
can and do change positions. It is important to extend the network of relationships, codify the procedures, ensure an active board of community participants, and to take steps that allow new individuals with different perspectives
to take on major responsibilities. Also, although a university's involvement
can often be coordinated by one institute, it is also increasingly necessary to
bring central university administrators into the partnership in order to build
wider campus recognition and support for the effort. The activities at UC
Berkeley have expanded from a base in City and Regional Planning to a more
multidisciplinary group of faculty and students from almost all the professional schools and other departments, and there is also significant budgetary
support from the central administration.* (Rubin, pp. 309-310)

C. Flexibility

Description   The collaborative group remains open to varied ways of organizing itself and accomplishing its work.

Implications   • Collaborative groups need to be flexible both in their structure and in their methods.

• Communicating the need and expectation for flexibility is crucial at the outset of a collaborative effort.

• Monitoring the collaborative group to ensure it remains flexible is important, since groups often tend over time to solidify their norms in ways that constrain their thinking and their behavior.

Illustration   A 1990 study of successful collaborations in the child care field provides examples of the kind of flexibility that is needed.

It may be a flexible response to the collaboration's geographic environment (a collaboration in a rural, mountainous state holds meetings in alternative sections of the state to allow all members equal opportunity to attend at least half of the collaboration's meetings). It may be a creative way to address staffing shortages (a collaboration with local universities allows a child care agency to adequately staff its program with early education, nursing, social service, and food service students). It may be stretching resources to serve more than one purpose (a collaboration that receives corporate funding for its efforts to expand day care centers and homes to accommodate the needs of employees notes that this also increases the availability of child care for the public). Large accomplishments or small, collaborations report that flexible responses to their environment enable them to continue to pursue their goals. (Kagan et al., p. 43)

D. Development of clear roles and policy guidelines

Description   The collaborating partners clearly understand their roles, rights, and responsibilities, and they understand how to carry out those responsibilities.

Implications   • Members need to discuss the roles, rights, and responsibilities of the partners, reach agreement on these, and clearly communicate them to all relevant parties. Letters of agreement may be helpful.[15]

• Collaborating partners need to resolve any conflict resulting from the competition between demands placed on them as employees of the organization they represent and demands they face as members of a collaborative team. Participating organizations may need to adjust policies and procedures to reduce this conflict in roles.

---

[15] These could specify roles, rights, responsibilities, and procedures. They could also state the basic values and philosophy of the group. If possible, collaborating partners might have these letters developed and signed within every level of their organization (see Factor 3B, Multiple layers of participation).

- Role definitions should not be so rigid that they inhibit flexibility. For some collaborative groups, effective policy may entail the assignment of responsibilities on a situation-specific basis.

- Members' true interests and strengths should be considered when making assignments. Ultimately, people will gravitate toward their interest.

A 1995 study of collaboration between a Head Start program and a community health center emphasizes the need for clearly defined roles and procedures.

Illustration

When the on-site clinic opened, no one had given much thought as to who would make appointments and keep the appointment book. Initially, the family workers at the Clinton Avenue site were responsible for scheduling all clinic appointments for Head Start families and for scheduling non-Head Start families when the clinic was closed. As discussed earlier, this arrangement seemed on the surface to make sense because the clinic was open only limited hours, but family workers were always there, and because family services workers interacted with families frequently. This arrangement, however, burdened family workers, particularly with the heavy emphasis on outreach to draw more non-Head Start children to the clinic. They were worried about being overwhelmed by the workload of clinic scheduling. Through the fall meetings, the Leaguers and NCHC worked out a clearer definition of roles and shifted more responsibility for scheduling to the clinic staff. (Lukas and Weiss, p. 25)

E. Adaptability

The collaborative group has the ability to sustain itself in the midst of major changes, even if it needs to change some major goals, members, etc., in order to deal with changing conditions.[16]

Description

- A collaborative group should keep itself aware of community trends, other changes in the environment, and the directions pursued by its members. It should accommodate itself to these developments.

Implications

- The vision and goals of a collaborative group must be reviewed regularly and revised if appropriate.

- Since member goals and outcomes change, collaborative goals and outcomes need to keep pace by continually incorporating changes as necessary.

A 1980 study describes the adaptive process used by some collaborative groups in response to changes in external conditions.

Illustrations

While all the projects have in one manner or another implemented a school-to-work transition effort, it is also the case that, almost without exception, what now is in place is not entirely what was anticipated nor promised when the

---

[16] Flexibility (Factor 3C) and adaptability may appear similar. However, they refer to two different aspects of group process. Flexibility relates to means: the ability of a collaborative group to use different methods or structures, as needed, to meet the demands of a project. Adaptability relates to ends: the ability of a collaborative group to adjust its vision, fundamental goals, or philosophies as a result of new learnings or new conditions that have developed.

grant application was made. The process of improvisation and of continually readjusting the goals of the program to changing political, economic, and social conditions has resulted in efforts dissimilar to those initially envisioned. (Rist et al., p. xv)

A 1996 study describes the adaptive process used by a collaborative group that recognized it would likely fail to achieve its initial goals.

Another example of a shift in objective and goal direction was evidenced in the Vallejo Community Empowerment Project. This collaborative was initially directed toward educating and supporting teenage women and mothers in the community. When the collaborative realized they could not engage the teenage population in their efforts, they shifted their goals and direction toward community safety. This new direction brought in even more coordination and participation. (Rogers et al., p. 171)

F. Appropriate pace of development

Description

The structure, resources, and activities of the collaborative group change over time to meet the needs of the group without overwhelming its capacity, at each point throughout the initiative.[17]

Implications

- Experienced collaborative groups may be better prepared than newly established groups to handle the complexities of large-scale collaborative ventures.

- The number and diversity of collaborating partners should not be more than the collaboration requires or can support at any given time. The elimination of formerly needed partners, or the incorporation of new partners who would not have previously been appropriate, may sometimes be necessary.

- Attainment of small, short-term goals can help to cement trust and build relationships during the early stages of collaborative work. More ambitious goals can then be pursued in the context of a stable, well-established collaborative arrangement.

- Collaboration often requires different resource supplies at different times. Sufficient funding and staff time may be especially important during the start-up and implementation phases of a project.

James Austin (2000) suggests that in collaborations among organizations with different types of expertise (e.g., a nonprofit health organization collaborating with a nonprofit children's day care organization, or a for-profit business organization collaborating with a nonprofit arts organization), the need to "renew value" may occur cyclically. That is, after one organization has learned all that it feels it needs to know as of a certain time, its interest in continuing to collaborate may begin to wane. To deal with this predictable phenomenon (if

---

[17] This factor is new to the 2001 edition.

it truly does occur commonly in some types of collaborations), collaborating partners may need to take steps to reinforce success factors such as self-interest, shared vision, and others at certain points throughout their work.

The benefits of incremental growth are described in a 1997 study of an interagency service network designed to prevent child abuse and neglect. The network was established as a collaboration between seven private nonprofits, and expanded to incorporate a public school only after the original agencies had learned to work effectively with one another.

Starting small helped create a manageable scale of relationships that facilitated the timely joint action needed to produce multiple and integrated services in a time-limited project. Starting small also gave partners the opportunity to be innovative in the development of the prototype network, and their nonprofit status provided flexibility and adaptive efficiency in refining the model. Bonds were developed and strengthened among existing and community-based agencies in close proximity that had not previously worked together. (Mulroy, pp. 262-263)

Illustration

4. Factors Related to COMMUNICATION

Communication refers to the channels used by collaborative partners to send and receive information, keep one another informed, and convey opinions to influence the group's actions.

A. Open and frequent communication

Collaborative group members interact often, update one another, discuss issues openly, and convey all necessary information to one another and to people outside the group.

Description

- Setting up a system of communication at the beginning of a collaborative effort, and identifying the responsibilities each member has for communication, will greatly enhance the group's efforts.

Implications

- A staff function for communication may be necessary, depending upon the size and complexity of the collaborative group.

- There should be incentives within and among organizations to encourage effective communication and discourage ineffective communication.

- Communications strategies must be planned to reflect the diverse communications styles of the members of the collaborative group.

- Collaborators need to acknowledge that problems will occur and that they must be communicated. Conflict is often good, and there will be topics on which collaborators may "agree to disagree."

- Selective distribution of oral and written communication must be avoided since this might splinter the group.

Illustration

A 1999 study provides examples of how frequent communication increased the success of a collaborative research project in which partners designed, implemented, and evaluated a workplace-based domestic abuse prevention program.

To be inclusive, information must flow in all directions. To be efficient, the flow must be directed and rapid. The research design and success of its implementation depends on finding effective ways to hear the many voices of the collaboration efficiently and effectively. Creating a mechanism for including information efficiently requires planning. For example, as items on the survey were based directly on the training outline and were designed to measure if the training affected employees' attitudes and intended behaviors, changes in the [Domestic Abuse Program] training material had to be communicated to the evaluators. This required close coordination and communication between the researchers and program developers. Feedback was funneled through the project coordinator, who then contacted the evaluators with any changes. (Urban and Bennett, p. 1189)

B. Established informal relationships and communication links

Description

In addition to formal channels of communication, members establish personal connections—producing a better, more informed, and cohesive group working on a common project.

Implications

- Stable representation from collaborating organizations is needed to develop strong personal connections. If representatives "turn over" too rapidly, or differ from meeting to meeting, strong links will not develop.

- Communication efforts such as meetings, trainings, and interagency work groups should promote understanding, cooperation, and transfer of information.

- Setting aside purely social time might be helpful for members of a collaborative group.

- Members will need to review systems and procedures regularly to upgrade and expand communications.

- Relying too much on the paper process won't be healthy; members need to get to know each other.

Illustration

In an examination of university involvement in community-building initiatives, a 1998 study found that collaboration was enhanced by the existence of long-standing personal connections among individual staff members.

Continuity of involvement is important to both the community and the university. The activities that the University-Oakland Metropolitan Forum undertook through its HUD-supported projects did not begin with an application for federal support. Rather, they were the consequence of the Forum's previous eight years of building institutional and personal connections and credibility, and of service to community groups and local government. Several key individuals were involved in these university-community relationships for the entire decade, even as they changed jobs. Nearly a dozen former students who worked at the Forum, dating back to 1990, are now staff members in the city and in nonprofit organizations who supervise student interns and negotiate with the university about the next round of activities. As a result, when new needs or opportunities arise, they can be addressed through an informal network of connections among the university, community organizations, and local government. (Rubin, p. 309)

5. Factors Related to PURPOSE

Purpose refers to the reasons for the development of a collaborative effort, the result or vision the collaborative group seeks, and the specific tasks or projects the collaborative group defines as necessary to accomplish. It is driven by a need, crisis, or opportunity.

A. Concrete, attainable goals and objectives

Goals and objectives of the collaborative group are clear to all partners, and can realistically be attained.

Description

- Goals lacking clarity or attainability will diminish enthusiasm; clear, attainable goals will heighten enthusiasm.

Implications

- Collaborative groups must experience a progression of "successes" during the collaborative process in order to be sustained. Defining success too narrowly and distantly—only by accomplishing the collaboration's ultimate goals—can be discouraging.

- At the outset, collaborative groups should formulate clear goals, then periodically report on progress.

- Success will be more likely if a collaborative group develops both short- and long-term goals.

The university-community collaborative project in a 1997 study found success by focusing on concrete, attainable goals.

Illustration

To overcome early skepticism and suspicion, the university had to demonstrate that it could be a valuable partner by directly assisting the community organization with its current needs. Likewise, the community organization had to be prepared to utilize the services and resources made available by the university and to direct the effort in a productive and efficient manner. Working on real projects that lead to tangible results with positive outcomes is what demonstrates the value of the partnership to each partner. At the same time, actual collaboration (rather than just talking about it) strengthens individual relationships, establishes clear lines of communication between the organizations, and engenders the trust that is the basis for ongoing collaborations. (Wiewel and Guerrero, p. 126)

B. Shared vision

Description

Collaborating partners have the same vision, with clearly agreed-upon mission, objectives, and strategy. The shared vision may exist at the outset of collaboration, or the partners may develop a vision as they work together.

Implications

- A collaborative group must develop a shared vision either when the collaboration is first planned, or soon after it begins to function.

- The shared vision may motivate collaborating partners to resolve conflicts and work persistently toward common goals.

- Members will need to engage in vision-building efforts and develop a language and actions out of the shared vision.

- Technical assistance (outside consultation) may be useful to establish the common vision.

- Any imbalances of power among collaborating partners must be addressed openly. These imbalances should not be allowed to stop the group from developing a truly shared vision.

Illustration

A 1991 study of states that implemented coordinated services for families with a handicapped child discussed the importance of a shared vision.

A vision of the desired service system, which is shared by multiple persons in several centers of influence is critical to progress. Three of the six states studied had shared vision as an "extremely strong" enabling factor. Progress also appeared to be related to the sharing of this vision across four to five agencies, organizations, power sources, and constituencies. An important part of the vision also is a set of administrative and political strategies by which the state can move from its current position to the desired vision. (Harbin et al., p. 11)

C. Unique purpose

Description

The mission and goals, or approach, of the collaborative group differ, at least in part, from the mission and goals, or approach, of the member organizations.

Implications

- The mission and goals of a collaborative group must create a "sphere of activity." This sphere may overlap with but should not be identical to the sphere of any member organization.[18]

- The mission and goals of collaborative members need to be known by all involved.

- Collaboration among competing organizations to achieve goals each member already works toward may lead to failure. Less demanding attempts to coordinate or cooperate might fare better.

---

[18] Van de Ven (1976) suggests that an optimal range probably exists. The purpose of a collaborative group must be sufficiently close to the purpose of member organizations to make membership attractive. However, if it duplicates exactly the purpose of any member organization, that organization will not participate and may even attempt to subvert the collaboration.

In a 1998 study of nine neighborhood-based collaborative groups, members reported experiencing tension when the group's activities too closely resembled those of the partner organizations.

Turf issues surfaced in a number of ways. Many [community-based development organizations] felt threatened when they saw another organization doing work similar to their own, or they would actively oppose a joint undertaking by the collaborative if they perceived it as competing with their own projects. (Pitt, p. 18)

Illustration

6. Factors Related to RESOURCES

Resources include financial and human "input" necessary to develop and sustain a collaborative group.

A. Sufficient funds, staff, materials, and time

The collaborative group has an adequate, consistent financial base, along with the staff and materials needed to support its operations. It allows sufficient time to achieve its goals and includes time to nurture the collaboration.

Description

- Obtaining the financial means for existence must be a priority in forming a collaborative group.

Implications

- Collaborative work may be expensive in the start-up phase. Money should be available at the outset.

- Collaboration is facilitated by flexible funding streams, which permit the application of resources to projects involving diverse issues and organizations.

- A collaborative group needs to consider the resources of its members as well as the necessity of approaching outside sources.

- In-kind support is as valuable as dollars.

- Staff time and skills are essential to collaborative success. Partner organizations must be prepared to devote substantial staff hours to the collaboration.

- The collaborative process should not be rushed. Solid relationships take time to develop, and goals are more easily attained when pursued with patience and persistence.

A 1999 study of successful collaborative research highlights the kinds of obstacles that must be overcome when a collaborative group fails to arrange for an adequate supply of resources.

Illustration

If collaboration is a priority, the project must allocate considerable time, energy, and resources to maintain it. Otherwise, the collaboration may not be effective or even continue to exist. This is true at every stage of the project.

Planning for the [Chicago Women's Health Risk Study] underestimated the amount of resources that would be required to maintain the collaboration. Competition for scarce resources became a problem. Staff began to think of time spent on maintaining collaboration as conflicting with time spent on furthering research goals. For example, because communication is key to many of the values inherent in the collaborative culture, and communication requires resources, research staff kept and distributed detailed minutes of each meeting and made a special effort to contact anyone who had missed a meeting. Each contact was a conscious attempt to share information and to reinforce the partnership. On a given day, however, staff might have to choose between handling a site protocol or respondent safety issue and writing up the minutes of the last general meeting. (Block et al., pp. 1167-1168)

B. Skilled leadership

Description

The individual who provides leadership for the collaborative group has organizing and interpersonal skills, and carries out the role with fairness. Because of these characteristics (and others), the leader is granted respect or "legitimacy" by the collaborative partners.

Implications

- In selecting the collaborative group leader, care must be taken to find a person who has process skills, a good image, and knowledge of the subject area.

- Leaders of collaborative groups must give serious attention and care to their role.

- The grooming of new leaders and planning for transitions in leadership should be well-thought-out to avoid costly power struggles and loss of forward momentum.

- A convener should be skilled at maintaining a balance between process and task activities; and a convener should enable all members to maintain their roles within the collaborative group.

Illustration

Effective leadership was critical to the establishment of a collaborative program to educate homeless children, as documented in a 1993 study.

The ACP board president has always been of pivotal importance. The first board president also served as the principal of ACP and its sister school. Wearing two hats, she was able to develop relationships in the joint effort, exercise leadership from both positions, and communicate with the school system about ACP's development and needs. Remaining on the board after the completion of her term, she continued to have a strong commitment to the initiative's success. The second board president, a minister, resigned after a very stressful period for ACP, chiefly caused by personnel problems, but exacerbated by the board's lack of a clear vision. The third president, a pediatrician and child advocate, took over and guided the program through its rather shaky second year and on to solid ground by the end of the third year. Her strength was the ability to keep the board focused on its goals and help clarify its vision and purpose. (Yon et al., p. 418)

CHAPTER 4

Putting the Factors to Work

THE FIRST edition of *Collaboration: What Makes It Work*, published in 1992, has helped others to take great strides both in collaboration practice and in collaboration research. A primary goal of that publication was to offer a useful reference that would improve collaboration, when people choose to do it. Collaboration is only a tool, and like any tool, it works well only when applied to an appropriate task. If an organization decides to collaborate with one or more other organizations, then the more the partners include the twenty factors as ingredients in their work, the greater the likelihood that they will succeed with their efforts.

During the decade of the 1990s, many organizations translated their knowledge of the success factors into practice, and many researchers used the first edition as one of the building blocks for their work.

The first edition also sought to codify research findings on collaboration—to help other researchers advance more rapidly than would be possible without such codification, and to avoid instances of researchers' reinventing the wheel because they didn't have access to what others had already discovered. In providing this service to the research community, the work became part of the expanding scientific endeavor of research synthesis or *meta-analysis*.[19]

In this edition, we can happily and proudly report that, during the decade of the 1990s, many organizations translated their knowledge of the success factors into practice, and many researchers used the first edition as one of the building blocks for their work.[20]

This chapter briefly mentions some of the organizations that have used the 1992 publication. Many of these organizations distributed information from that publication widely to their members in the United States and countries throughout the world. The chapter then reviews some of the research progress that others have made by drawing on the first edition of this work. Some researchers have found the distinctions between

---

[19] See, for example: Cooper and Hedges (1994); Cook et al. (1992); Wachter and Straf (1990).

[20] As of last count, the Wilder Publishing Center (now Fieldstone Alliance) had granted permission for reprints of sections of the book some forty-two times in print, web, and other forms.

cooperation, coordination, and collaboration useful in thinking about the partnerships they've analyzed; others have used the success factors as a basis for new studies. We conclude the chapter by mentioning some questions that remain to be answered.

Collaboration Practice

Wendall Walls, of the Greenleaf Center for Servant Leadership, stated that the first edition of *Collaboration: What Makes It Work* "provided a lens" through which to view a collaborative initiative between the Greenleaf Center and the National Association for Community Leadership.[21] Walls characterized this initiative as something akin to a leadership process, cocreated by the partners, in which they "develop a shared vision, set a direction, solve problems, and make meaning of their work." In a succinct description and commentary on his work, including suggestions on relationship building, communication, clarifying expectations, and so on, he provides practical advice on how collaborating partners can build the factors for success into their projects.

The American Cancer Society made extensive use of the 1992 edition when it developed a packet of materials on collaboration for its units throughout the United States. The materials, prepared by the National Advisory Group on Collaboration with Organizations, present a philosophy, principles, and guidelines for collaboration, along with some practical worksheets based on the nineteen factors.

The Pew Charitable Trusts created a special listing of the factors from the first edition of *Collaboration: What Makes It Work* in its publication *Building Collaborative Communities*.[22] The Pew publication sought to "provide practical approaches for the development of stronger, more effective communities" and to "encourage conversation about our shared civic life." The report emphasizes that collaboration requires care, both to initiate it productively and to sustain its health over time. It requires that people abandon turf and, often, that they assume a different way of thinking and acting.

The Pew report offers jazz as a metaphor for collaboration. Jazz occurs in a social setting, requiring partners. Similar to collaboration, it expects a willingness among the partners to take a theme and play with it, constructing something of value. In addition, quoting jazz trumpeter Wynton Marsalis, "Playing jazz means learning how to reconcile differences, even when they're opposites…. Jazz teaches you how to have dialogue with integrity."

The American Association of Homes and Services for the Aging routinely made *Collaboration: What Makes It Work* available to its members during the 1990s.

The Community National Outcome Work Group, at the University of Arizona, extensively used the first edition of *Collaboration: What Makes It Work* to develop advice on how communities can develop resources and increase "social capital."

---

[21] See Walls (2000).

[22] See Morse (1996).

Representatives of countries in Eastern Europe and within the former Soviet Union have reported to us that they received the book from international aid organizations and that they found it very useful. Organizations in Northern Ireland found the book helpful in promoting and planning collaboration.

The Center for Ocean Sciences Education Excellence used the first edition of *Collaboration: What Makes It Work* as a basis for asserting the need to formulate a systematic strategy for collaboration among educational institutions to promote ocean science curriculum development.[23]

The Drucker Foundation listed *Collaboration: What Makes It Work* as recommended reading for those interested in improving their communities.

A strategic health care consulting group, Arista, used the factors from the first edition of *Collaboration: What Makes It Work* to develop a tool for its clients to use for analyzing their collaborative efforts.

The Community Works Tool Box used the definition of collaboration and the success factors on its website to assist community organizations that want to collaborate.

Other initiatives that have incorporated the factors into their collaborative work include state agencies, schools, and networks of health care facilities.

Many groups have reported to us the valuable experience they had assessing their collaborative initiative on the basis of the factors influencing success. Groups have done this prior to beginning a collaborative, during the course of collaboration, or both. Chapter Five presents The Wilder Collaboration Factors Inventory, a tool for this purpose, and describes how some groups have used this inventory.

Collaboration Research

Many researchers have built upon the findings in *Collaboration: What Makes It Work* or have used the publication as a framework for their research. This has helped to systematize the research on collaboration, rendering it more productive as researchers advance on previous discoveries, use common vocabulary when appropriate, and recognize the similarities and differences across their individual endeavors.

Some of this work has provided additional confirmation of the factors. The research synthesis in this second edition includes that work.

Other researchers have found the 1992 publication useful for their analyses of joint efforts that may not technically constitute full-fledged collaboration.

---

[23] See Center for Ocean Sciences Education Excellence (2000).

Kerka (1997) provided research-based recommendations in a Practice Application Brief produced for the ERIC Clearinghouse on Adult, Career, and Vocational Education. She used the categories and factors from *Collaboration: What Makes It Work* as a central piece in her recommendations.

Research that has used the first edition of *Collaboration: What Makes It Work*—whether to study collaborative initiatives or other forms of joint work—includes, for example:

- Aronstein and Connolly (1999) used *Collaboration: What Makes It Work* to analyze a cross-sector partnership and linked several of the nineteen factors to its success. They conclude that the book offers a useful model for talking about collaborative initiatives and identifying areas for improvement.

- Harbert et al. (1997) point to two difficulties in the evaluation of interagency efforts. First, "it is not always clear what type of interagency actions are being studied" and, second, there is a "lack of a definitive framework for evaluating this type of interagency effort." The authors draw on Wilder's explication of cooperation, coordination, and collaboration in response to the first problem, suggesting that the distinctions among these levels of partnership are useful in assessing interagency relationships.

  Harbert et al. also discuss their study of a collaborative children's initiative. Based on their assessment of the factors that influence the success of collaboration, the authors conclude that the absence of two factors led to the failure of that collaborative effort to move into an implementation phase (thereby becoming a "true collaboration" and succeeding according to the authors' definition of success).

  Finally, Harbert et al. note that outcomes to be expected from successful collaboration are different at different phases. Successful completion of the formative phase would entail development of a strategic action plan and a move into the implementation phase. This relates to the "appropriate pace of development" factor identified in this second edition.

- Dayton et al. (1997) also use the Mattessich and Monsey definitions to identify their case as one of coordination and discuss its success.

- O'Donnell et al. (1998) found the nineteen success factors useful in looking at partnerships between agencies and community residents.

The studies noted above used the 1992 compilation of collaboration success factors as a research tool. These studies demonstrate how researchers can build upon previous work in their field to produce research that both stands on a solid scientific foundation and provides practical findings that people doing collaboration can apply in their efforts. We hope that more researchers adopt this approach—to do high-quality research that has implications for practice and that is reported in a clear way, using standard vocabulary that does not require extensive deciphering in order to apply to real-world tasks.

Opportunities for Future Research

Many opportunities exist for further study of collaboration. For example:

- Can we discover additional evidence to confirm the importance of each factor?

- What is the relative importance of each factor? Can we assign a "weight" to each, indicating different levels of attention that each deserves? Aronstein and Connolly (1999) conclude that an appropriate mix of some factors is critically important to attain among collaborations working in turbulent or unpredictable political environments.

- Are some factors more important at certain stages of a collaboration or for certain types of groups? The research of the last eight years led to the addition of "appropriate pace of development" as a success factor in the present edition of this work, suggesting that differences may exist in the importance of some factors, depending upon the stage in which the partners find themselves.

- Related to "pace of development," are there certain factors that must be present at a certain level, by a certain point in a collaborative relationship—such that they create a "fork in the road" for the collaborating groups? That is, if they are not present, should a collaborative effort be postponed or terminated?

- What are the most effective ways to build success factors into collaborative arrangements? Even when the factors are recognized as important, their cultivation in practice is often not straightforward.[24]

- Can we "dig more deeply" to understand what produces the presence or absence of success factors in specific initiatives? For example, a lack of mutual respect, understanding, and trust may result from negative attitudes; lack of understanding due to technical jargon of different organizations; philosophical differences among partners; different organizational styles for accomplishing tasks, dealing with staff, and other important matters; and differences in community norms related to culture or race (suggested by Karasoff, 1998).

- What are the costs and benefits of collaboration? Do the benefits outweigh the costs, or vice versa, in certain types of situations, or for certain types of groups? Is it possible to assess the net gains of collaboration?

- What factors influence whether people will come together at all (pre-collaborative stage)?

- Does the history or "prehistory" of collaborative initiatives influence the way the factors develop or their relative importance? (For example, do differences exist between mandated and voluntary collaborative arrangements?)

- What about long-term outcomes? Not much research has followed collaborative initiatives beyond the point where initial success can be assessed.

---

[24] Huxham and Vangen (1996, 2000) make this point in their in-depth discussion of membership, goal definition, compromise, communication, and trust.

An Important Question: When Should Organizations Collaborate?

Both researchers and practitioners need to analyze and articulate the situations in which collaboration does and does not offer an appropriate tool. In our opinion, the past decade has included "collaboration mania" among some people who set policy and offer funding. Unfortunately, it has also become a nostrum among some non-profit organizations desperate to attempt anything to survive in a challenging environment. The foundations and government agencies that have promoted the wise use of collaboration need to serve as examples for all of us as we strive to address important issues and accomplish important work in the most effective ways.

Collaboration does not always constitute the best way to accomplish tasks or address issues, any more than a pair of pliers always serves as the best tool for household repairs.

Collaboration is a tool for achieving something of value. It is not an end in and of itself. Collaboration does not always constitute the best way to accomplish tasks or address issues, any more than a pair of pliers always serves as the best tool for household repairs. Forms of organizational partnership other than collaboration may be appropriate in many situations. Engaging in various other forms of partnership may also be a valuable first step on the road to "true" collaboration.[25]

In fact, organizations may cooperate, coordinate, collaborate, even merge, to accomplish goals. All of these may be considered in the attempt to fulfill a mission. Those who feel that joint efforts offer promise for getting important work done always need to assess the pros and cons of alternative arrangements to determine which will best suit their needs at a particular time. They should then develop their strategy to construct the best arrangement of partners—whether that entails collaboration or something else.

---

[25] See Harbert et al. (1997). In addition, Ashman (2000) asserts on the basis of her study that for civil society-business partnerships no difference exists in levels of success between resource-based and strategic partnerships (the latter entailing more intense involvement by all partners).

CHAPTER 5

Examining Your Own Collaborative Project

THIS CHAPTER describes how you can use The Wilder Collaboration Factors Inventory, an instrument that has helped many groups to examine where they stand on the factors that influence the success of collaboration.

Wilder Research Center staff developed and revised this inventory. They have tested it with a variety of groups during the eight years since publication of the first edition of *Collaboration: What Makes It Work*.[26] The inventory helps groups to do a systematic, careful examination of where they stand on the factors that influence the success of collaboration. Groups can use this instrument to develop a list, or "inventory," of their strengths and weaknesses with respect to the factors that influence collaborative success. Note, however, that the inventory does *not* provide a single numerical index or score on the overall potential of a group to succeed with collaboration. It has not been developed as a measure with validity and reliability established through psychometric research.[27] It provides information that groups can use as a starting point for discussion.

The Wilder Collaboration Factors Inventory can be applied anytime before or during a collaborative initiative's life. If a group has just begun to consider a collaborative initiative, it can use the inventory results to assess its readiness to collaborate. If the results point to weaknesses, the group can remedy those *before* they grow into major

---

[26] Greg Owen and Barbara Monsey developed the first version of The Wilder Collaboration Factors Inventory, with assistance from Paul Mattessich. Marta Murray-Close revised the inventory for this publication, again assisted by Paul Mattessich. No records exist to indicate how many groups have used the inventory, but we know that it has been requested by a large number of groups throughout the United States and in some other countries. Some of those groups have reported back to us with comments that were used for improvement.

[27] It is impossible, given the nature of the inventory, to give definitive interpretations of numerical scores. Groups need to set their own standards. The scoring method presented in this chapter offers a general approach to interpreting your group's results, but it should be viewed more as a starting point for discussion than as a conclusive statement about your likelihood of success.

obstacles. If a group has already begun an initiative, it can use the inventory to assess the strengths and weaknesses of its collaborative activities, and then take steps to address the weaknesses.

The inventory focuses attention on each factor and leads people to think about the relationships among collaborating partners as well as about their own organizations.

Purchasers of *Collaboration: What Makes It Work, Second Edition,* may photocopy this inventory for use only with their collaboration. Separate copies of the inventory, designed for easy distribution to individual members of the collaboration, are also available from Fieldstone Alliance; see ordering information at the back of this book.

The Wilder Collaboration Factors Inventory

This questionnaire can help your group inventory its strengths on the factors that research has shown are important for the success of collaborative projects. The questionnaire is designed for use by people who are planning or participating in collaborative projects.

There are no right or wrong answers. Your opinion is important, even if it is very different from the opinions of others. When your group sees the results, you all will learn how people feel—whether they all feel the same or different about the questions.

Unless your group has decided to put names on the questionnaires, your answers will not be associated with your name and will be grouped with the answers of others.

Instructions

Please follow the instructions *exactly*. They are very simple:

1. Read each item.
2. Circle the number that indicates how much you agree or disagree with each item.
3. Do not skip any items.
4. Return your form as instructed by your group leader or facilitator.

You might want to do something a bit differently, but we have learned from experience that your group will get the most benefit if you fill out the questionnaire as the instructions describe. Some special situations:

"Don't know"

If you feel you don't know how to answer an item, or that you don't have an opinion, circle the "neutral" response, the number 3.

Opinion falls "in between two numbers"

If you feel that your opinion lies in between two numbers, pick the lower of the two. Do not put a mark in between the two numbers; and do not circle both of them. For example, if you feel your opinion lies between 1 and 2, circle the 1.

The Wilder Collaboration Factors Inventory was developed by Wilder Research Center and is distributed by Fieldstone Alliance, to accompany *Collaboration: What Makes It Work.* Purchasers of *Collaboration: What Makes It Work, Second Edition,* may photocopy this inventory *for use only with their collaboration.* Separate copies of the inventory, professionally packaged and designed for distribution to members of the collaboration, are also available from Fieldstone Alliance; see ordering information at the back of this book. Because these preprinted inventories include substantial information about each of the factors, many groups find them more useful for spurring group discussion than simply photocopying the inventory from this book. Groups who use the instrument (in either form) are encouraged to notify Wilder Research Center in order to list their use and to become part of the mailing list for future updates or notices. Address: Wilder Research Center, 451 Lexington Parkway North, Saint Paul, Minnesota 55104, U.S.A. E-mail: research@wilder.org

The Wilder Collaboration Factors Inventory

_____   _____
Name of Collaboration Project   *Date*

If you have been asked to provide your name or the name of your organization, please do so below.

_____   _____
Respondent Name   *Organization*

Include your name or the name of your organization on the line above only if instructed to do so.

Statements about Your Collaborative Group

Factor	Statement	Strongly Disagree	Disagree	Neutral, No Opinion	Agree	Strongly Agree
History of collaboration or cooperation in the community	1. Agencies in our community have a history of working together.	1	2	3	4	5
	2. Trying to solve problems through collaboration has been common in this community. It's been done a lot before.	1	2	3	4	5
Collaborative group seen as a legitimate leader in the community	3. Leaders in this community who are not part of our collaborative group seem hopeful about what we can accomplish.	1	2	3	4	5
	4. Others (in this community) who are not part of this collaboration would generally agree that the organizations involved in this collaborative project are the "right" organizations to make this work.	1	2	3	4	5
Favorable political and social climate	5. The political and social climate seems to be "right" for starting a collaborative project like this one.	1	2	3	4	5
	6. The time is right for this collaborative project.	1	2	3	4	5
Mutual respect, understanding, and trust	7. People involved in our collaboration always trust one another.	1	2	3	4	5
	8. I have a lot of respect for the other people involved in this collaboration.	1	2	3	4	5
Appropriate cross section of members	9. The people involved in our collaboration represent a cross section of those who have a stake in what we are trying to accomplish.	1	2	3	4	5
	10. All the organizations that we need to be members of this collaborative group have become members of the group.	1	2	3	4	5
Members see collaboration as in their self-interest	11. My organization will benefit from being involved in this collaboration.	1	2	3	4	5

Factor	Statement	Strongly Disagree	Disagree	Neutral, No Opinion	Agree	Strongly Agree
Ability to compromise	12. People involved in our collaboration are willing to compromise on important aspects of our project.	1	2	3	4	5
Members share a stake in both process and outcome	13. The organizations that belong to our collaborative group invest the right amount of time in our collaborative efforts.	1	2	3	4	5
	14. Everyone who is a member of our collaborative group wants this project to succeed.	1	2	3	4	5
	15. The level of commitment among the collaboration participants is high.	1	2	3	4	5
Multiple layers of participation	16. When the collaborative group makes major decisions, there is always enough time for members to take information back to their organizations to confer with colleagues about what the decision should be.	1	2	3	4	5
	17. Each of the people who participate in decisions in this collaborative group can speak for the entire organization they represent, not just a part.	1	2	3	4	5
Flexibility	18. There is a lot of flexibility when decisions are made; people are open to discussing different options.	1	2	3	4	5
	19. People in this collaborative group are open to different approaches to how we can do our work. They are willing to consider different ways of working.	1	2	3	4	5
Development of clear roles and policy guidelines	20. People in this collaborative group have a clear sense of their roles and responsibilities.	1	2	3	4	5
	21. There is a clear process for making decisions among the partners in this collaboration.	1	2	3	4	5
Adaptability	22. This collaboration is able to adapt to changing conditions, such as fewer funds than expected, changing political climate, or change in leadership.	1	2	3	4	5
	23. This group has the ability to survive even if it had to make major changes in its plans or add some new members in order to reach its goals.	1	2	3	4	5
Appropriate pace of development	24. This collaborative group has tried to take on the right amount of work at the right pace.	1	2	3	4	5
	25. We are currently able to keep up with the work necessary to coordinate all the people, organizations, and activities related to this collaborative project.	1	2	3	4	5

Factor	Statement	Strongly Disagree	Disagree	Neutral, No Opinion	Agree	Strongly Agree
Open and frequent communication	26. People in this collaboration communicate openly with one another.	1	2	3	4	5
	27. I am informed as often as I should be about what goes on in the collaboration.	1	2	3	4	5
	28. The people who lead this collaborative group communicate well with the members.	1	2	3	4	5
Established informal relationships and communication links	29. Communication among the people in this collaborative group happens both at formal meetings and in informal ways.	1	2	3	4	5
	30. I personally have informal conversations about the project with others who are involved in this collaborative group.	1	2	3	4	5
Concrete, attainable goals and objectives	31. I have a clear understanding of what our collaboration is trying to accomplish.	1	2	3	4	5
	32. People in our collaborative group know and understand our goals.	1	2	3	4	5
	33. People in our collaborative group have established reasonable goals.	1	2	3	4	5
Shared vision	34. The people in this collaborative group are dedicated to the idea that we can make this project work.	1	2	3	4	5
	35. My ideas about what we want to accomplish with this collaboration seem to be the same as the ideas of others.	1	2	3	4	5
Unique purpose	36. What we are trying to accomplish with our collaborative project would be difficult for any single organization to accomplish by itself.	1	2	3	4	5
	37. No other organization in the community is trying to do exactly what we are trying to do.	1	2	3	4	5
Sufficient funds, staff, materials, and time	38. Our collaborative group has adequate funds to do what it wants to accomplish.	1	2	3	4	5
	39. Our collaborative group has adequate "people power" to do what it wants to accomplish.	1	2	3	4	5
Skilled leadership	40. The people in leadership positions for this collaboration have good skills for working with other people and organizations.	1	2	3	4	5

Scoring Your Group on the Factors That Influence Collaborative Success

The calculation of scores can rely upon the judgment of one person, a few people, or many people. In most cases, "the more the merrier." A greater number of raters will produce a more reliable result, and one that reflects the many different perspectives that individuals bring into a group.

In our experience, almost all groups have wanted to tabulate the inventory results quickly, by hand. They have not wanted to key the questionnaire into a data file for computer analysis.* The instructions and examples that we provide assume that you as well will want to manually tabulate the results.

When all raters have completed their inventories, the group's score for each factor can be calculated using the following steps:

1) Add together all the ratings for the items related to each factor.

2) Divide by the total number of ratings for those items. (This number is equal to the number of raters multiplied by the number of items for the factor.)

These two steps yield an average score for each factor.

Example:

Three raters complete The Wilder Collaboration Factors Inventory and want to know where their group stands in terms of "Flexibility." They consult the questionnaire and see that items eighteen and nineteen relate to this factor. Their individual ratings for these items are as follows:

	Item 18	Item 19
Rater 1	4	2
Rater 2	5	2
Rater 3	3	3

The raters follow steps (1) and (2) to yield an average score of 3.2 for "flexibility."

(1) $4 + 5 + 3 + 2 + 2 + 3 = 19$

(2) $19/6 = 3.2$

Note that all factors do not have the same number of questions. For example, "Ability to compromise" has only one question, while "Members share a stake in both process and outcome" has three questions. You will need to change the divisor in step (2) above to match the number of ratings for each factor.

To calculate scores on collaboration success factors as rated by the representatives of a specific organization within a collaborative group, simply follow steps (1) and (2) using only the ratings of individuals from the organization of interest. That is, add together all of the ratings by individuals from that organization and divide by the total number of ratings added.

---

* You can also score this inventory online at www.FieldstoneAlliance.org.

Interpreting Your Scores

The Wilder Collaboration Factors Inventory does not have normative standards that would enable you to construct definitive interpretations of numerical scores for the factors. Instead, your scores on the inventory can be used as a basis for constructive discussion and planning for your collaborative initiative.

As a general rule, we would say:

> Scores of *4.0 or higher* show a strength and probably don't need special attention.
>
> Scores from *3.0 to 3.9* are borderline and should be discussed by the group to see if they deserve attention.
>
> Scores of *2.9 or lower* reveal a concern and should be addressed.

Here are some other things to consider when reviewing your results:

1) **What are the strengths and weaknesses of the collaborative group with respect to the factors that influence collaborative success?**

   While your scores on The Wilder Collaboration Factors Inventory do not describe your standing on the factors in absolute terms, they can serve as a relative indicator of your readiness to collaborate. Consider the three or four highest-rated factors for your organization, and for the group as a whole; these high-rated factors may represent strengths that your group can draw on to sustain collaboration, even in the face of major challenges. Similarly, the three or four lowest-rated factors may represent problem areas that your organization and collaborative group should take steps to address.

2) **Do representatives from all organizations in the collaborative group tend to rate the factors the same way? If not, what are the implications?**

   If you can, you should look not just at the scores on the factors as rated by the total group, but also at the scores as rated by each organization. If you see variances, the group should ask why these variances exist.

   Sometimes, an organization that sees things differently can provide valuable insight to the rest of the group. The representatives from that organization can lead the group to a very helpful new understanding of its strengths and weaknesses. For example, an organization that gives ratings much higher or lower than other organizations on "Skilled leadership" may have an important perspective on the group's leader (e.g., her ability to manage projects, her fairness or honesty, her experience in similar situations) that other organizations ought to understand.

   Other times, an organization that sees the factors very differently from its partners may be having trouble participating or may be "out of the loop" for important communications and does not understand what is going on. If this is the case, the group might use this discovery as an opportunity to take corrective action before serious problems develop.

3) **For low-rated factors, are there particular items that are especially problematic?**

It may be helpful to examine responses for individual items related to your group's lowest-rated factors. For instance, your group may have received a low-average score for "Sufficient funds, staff, materials, and time" because the group does not appear to have adequate funds (very low score for item thirty-eight), in spite of the fact that they have enough personnel (good score for item thirty-nine). When individual items are problematic, it is more efficient and effective to remedy the specific deficiencies than to attempt to improve your standing on the general factor.

4) **How strong are your scores overall?**

Your scores on The Wilder Collaboration Factors Inventory are *not* an absolute reflection of your group's ability to collaborate effectively. We cannot tell you how high your scores must be on each factor to ensure success, nor can we tell you that scores below a certain level will inevitably lead to failure. However, your scores can be used as a basis for commonsense judgments about how to proceed with your collaboration.

As suggested earlier, scores of 4.0 or higher probably indicate strength on a factor; scores 2.9 or lower probably should raise concern in your group. Scores from 3.0 to 3.9 ought to prompt some discussion on your part, to determine if you need to devote attention to them.

Here is some general advice to cover some situations in which you might find yourself:

- If any score falls below 3.0, you should have the group discuss this as soon as possible. You should develop a plan to remedy whatever problem(s) exist if you wish to proceed with the collaboration.

- If most of your group's scores fall in the middle of the rating scale (3.0 to 3.9), you may need to take steps to improve your standing on several factors before proceeding.

- If most scores fall at 4.0 or above, and just a few fall between 3.0 and 3.9, you can probably be confident that your group has no major shortcomings.

No matter what, however, do not be lulled into complacency by good scores. The factors require ongoing maintenance. For example, just because communication is good at the outset of an initiative does not mean that it will continue to be so, unless the collaborating partners make an effort to keep up such communication.

Suggested Uses for The Wilder Collaboration Factors Inventory

Groups have used the inventory in the planning of a collaborative initiative as well as after collaboration has started. In some cases, just a small group of leaders or planners completed it; in other cases, a large number of representatives from collaborating organizations filled out questionnaires. This section describes different ways in which groups can use the inventory and offers some comments about them.

- **Use The Wilder Collaboration Factors Inventory to consider your group's likelihood of success before beginning collaborative work.**

  To estimate the probability that a newly formed collaborative will succeed, the group's steering or planning committee may find it useful to complete the Wilder Collaboration Factors Inventory before collaborative activity has begun, or at the very beginning of an initiative. This helps the committee to focus on the factors that influence collaborative success and allows members to assess their standing on each factor. Although members of a steering or planning committee represent a limited number of perspectives within a collaborative group, their ratings can shed light on potential barriers to success before valuable resources have been committed. When committee members feel that their joint effort scores low on a factor, they may take steps to remedy the deficiency prior to start-up or delay the beginning of their collaborative project.

- **Use the inventory at a large group meeting, as a springboard for discussion about the strengths and weaknesses of your collaborative venture.**

  When representatives of collaborating organizations meet, they can use The Wilder Collaboration Factors Inventory to facilitate effective discussion, planning, and management of their initiative. This can work at any point during the initiative. Time may be set aside as part of a meeting agenda for representatives to rate the partnership. Meeting attendees then complete the inventory individually, and factor scores are calculated for each partner organization and for the group as a whole, during the meeting. These scores provide data for discussion and direct members' attention to the current strong and weak points of their collaboration. The scores may also reveal differences in the ways that individual organizations rate the partnership. Use of the inventory in large group meetings has some drawbacks, in that it can be logistically difficult to administer the instrument and tally scores in a reasonable amount of time. Also problematic is the loss of input from those not present at the meeting. However, administering the inventory at group meetings provides a good way to get members talking about the strengths and weaknesses of their initiative. It encourages them to look at themselves individually and at the whole collaborative group, as part of overall planning for the initiative.

- **Mail the inventory to members of collaborating organizations and discuss the results at your next meeting.**

  Like administering it in group meetings, mailing The Wilder Collaboration Factors Inventory to members of partner organizations is a good way to solicit input from large numbers of people. This approach can also be used to assess a collaborative group's strengths and weaknesses at any point during the initiative. The chief advantage of a mailing is that it can include all relevant people, and is not as dependent on schedules as are meetings. A mailing allows individuals to complete the inventory independently, at their convenience. Scores can then be calculated prior to the meeting at which they are discussed. Mailed inventories may result in poor response rates, especially among busy people, and they do not lead to the immediate interaction and feedback that occur at meetings. Nonetheless, the results of mailings can act as catalysts for constructive discussion among members of a collaborative group.

A Case Example: Using The Wilder Collaboration Factors Inventory

The following example is based on the experience of a collaborative initiative whose members used the first edition of *Collaboration: What Makes It Work* to educate themselves about what is important for success. The case illustrates how one set of four organizations involved in a collaborative initiative assessed itself on the factors that influence collaborative success and used the results to take action to improve the likelihood of success. [28]

Background and Context

The Tulip County Public Health Department was a typical county health department, with personnel involved in some broad prevention work, compliance activities, and a small amount of public health nursing outreach. It had generally been successful in serving the people of Tulip County but, in early 1997, some employees of the department expressed concern that it was not adequately meeting the needs of the county's lower-income residents. These employees were particularly concerned about the department's reputation within the community, fearing that its image as an aloof and bureaucratic organization prevented it from reaching certain groups of residents.

The employees' concerns eventually led to a meeting at which key department staff discussed strategies for improving service to low-income residents of Tulip County. Meeting attendees eventually decided that, given the department's weak reputation among some groups, collaboration with community-based organizations would be an

---

[28] This example is based on a true case. However, names have been changed to preserve the anonymity of the organizations. In addition, some details have been added or modified either to preserve anonymity or to enhance the educational value of the illustration. At the time this collaborative group used the inventory, it only measured nineteen factors. For illustrative purposes, data on the new factor have been inserted. At last contact with this group, it continued to operate its collaborative initiative.

essential part of any successful approach to better service. For their next meeting, they invited two groups to attend: Sunny Side Health Collective and Neighbors Working Together.

Sunny Side Health Collective had a lot of experience providing health services in low-income areas of Tulip County. As a nonprofit organization in existence for more than ten years, it provided access to health care for uninsured and low-income families. Generally, neighborhood residents, other service providers, and funders perceived it as a very effective organization. Neighbors Working Together was a residents' organization with a good reputation within the community. It had a long history, kept alive by a few, core long-term members. Its number of active members varied, depending upon the perceived importance of issues in which it was involved. Politicians and others considered it a "must-involve" organization in community initiatives.

At the meeting with the health department, Sunny Side and Neighbors Working Together offered the observation that many low-income people were also new to the county and had special needs. They suggested that the group invite New Style, a small nonprofit organization in existence just three years, to participate in the collaborative. New Style specifically addressed the need for basic necessities among persons who had recently arrived in the neighborhood (housing referrals, food shelf, clothing, referrals to employment services).

Shortly thereafter, New Style was incorporated into the collaborative group. In July of 1997, the group applied for and received funding from a local foundation to develop a system for delivering counseling, information, and health services to families in one low-income neighborhood within Tulip County. The health department supplied additional funds for the project. The collaborative group also designated a project director for the initiative—a staff person from Sunny Side who had worked on getting the project designed and funded.

The collaborative initiative was intended to last at least three years. In October of 1997, as the project was just getting under way, the group held a planning retreat. In attendance were five representatives from Sunny Side, including the agency's executive director and the project director of the collaborative initiative. Other attendees included four representatives from the health department, six from Neighbors Working Together, and three from New Style. During the morning of the retreat, participants completed The Wilder Collaboration Factors Inventory. Wilder Research Center staff attended, tallied the group members' responses, and presented the results to the group for discussion. The following table summarizes the group's ratings for each of the twenty success factors.

Factor	Whole Group (18)	Sunny Side (5)	Tulip Co. PHD (4)	Neigh-bors (6)	New Style (3)
History of collaboration or cooperation in community	4.2	4.2	4.2	4.4	4.0
Collaborative group seen as a legitimate leader in the community	4.4	4.4	4.4	4.8	4.0
Favorable political and social climate	4.5	4.4	4.4	4.6	4.6
Mutual respect, understanding, and trust	3.3	4.0	3.4	3.2	2.7
Appropriate cross section of members	4.4	4.0	4.0	4.8	4.6
Members see collaboration as in their self-interest	4.5	4.8	4.5	4.6	4.0
Ability to compromise	4.3	4.4	4.0	4.5	4.4
Members share a stake in both process and outcome	4.4	4.4	4.4	4.8	4.0
Multiple layers of participation	4.6	4.8	4.5	4.5	4.6
Flexibility	4.4	4.2	4.5	4.5	4.4
Development of clear roles and policy guidelines	4.1	4.0	4.0	4.5	4.0
Adaptability	4.6	4.8	4.5	4.5	4.6
Appropriate pace of development	4.3	4.3	4.3	4.3	4.3
Open and frequent communication	4.4	4.6	4.0	4.4	4.4
Established informal relationships and communication links	2.4	2.4	2.5	2.4	2.1
Concrete, attainable goals and objectives	4.2	4.0	4.0	4.5	4.4
Shared vision	4.4	4.2	4.5	4.5	4.4
Unique purpose	4.0	4.6	2.5	4.5	4.2
Sufficient funds, staff, materials, and time	4.5	4.5	4.5	4.4	4.6
Skilled leadership	4.4	4.0	4.5	4.5	4.6

Interpretation of Results and Follow-up Decisions

The group discussed the above findings and drew several conclusions. First, participants at the retreat were happy to discover that, on the whole, the initiative was doing well with respect to the factors that influence collaborative success. Most factors received high-average scores and were viewed as strengths to be maintained, warranting no special attention. The factors listed below all received ratings equal to or exceeding 4.1, which participants considered acceptable. In addition, representatives from all four organizations gave relatively similar ratings for these factors.

- History of collaboration or cooperation in community
- Collaborative group seen as a legitimate leader in the community.
- Favorable political and social climate
- Appropriate cross section of members
- Members see collaboration as in their self-interest
- Ability to compromise
- Members share a stake in both process and outcome
- Multiple layers of participation
- Flexibility
- Development of clear roles and policy guidelines
- Adaptability
- Appropriate pace of development
- Open and frequent communication
- Concrete, attainable goals and objectives
- Shared vision
- Sufficient funds, staff, materials, and time
- Skilled leadership

While nearly all of the factors received positive ratings, participants at the retreat noted that ratings for "Mutual respect, understanding, and trust" suggested a possible weakness that needed to be explored. The average rating for this factor, 3.3, was considerably lower than the average ratings for most other factors. After much discussion, the group concluded that this rating was neither good enough to be acceptable nor bad enough to clearly demonstrate a weakness. It decided not to deal with this factor directly, reasoning that the partners had not been working together long enough to earn one another's trust. The participants believed that greater respect and understanding would develop among partners as the project progressed.

More problematic were the ratings for "Established informal relationships and communication links." This factor received an average rating of 2.4, the lowest rating for any factor. Participants at the retreat felt that this rating indicated a weakness that could jeopardize success and that needed immediate attention. Through discussion, they discovered that several people in each of the collaborating organizations felt "out of the loop." Some participants had the image, real or imagined, that decisions were sometimes made outside of regular channels and that they were not involved. Others felt that some people knew one another and would not hesitate to pick up the telephone and call one another, while others were barely acquainted with one another.

To deal with the issues raised, the group decided to try three actions and then assess how people felt several months later. First, it would arrange a social get-together during the next few weeks, with no agenda other than people getting to know one another. The group would also put time on formal meeting agendas for a bit of social conversation among participants. Finally, the partners agreed to rotate the site of their meetings, so that participants would feel more at home in one another's facilities.

Those present at the retreat also observed that the ratings for "Unique purpose," while high overall, were noticeably low from representatives of the public health department. The group decided to discuss the reasons why staff from the department had given this factor a lower rating than did the other participants at the retreat, in order to discover whether any problem or misunderstanding existed. It discovered that public health department staff had some concerns about whether the work of this group would overlap with other initiatives. Also, politicians had begun to exert more pressure on the department to "reduce duplication." Staff did not believe that duplication existed; in fact, they believed exactly the opposite, that the low-income population did not receive adequate service. However, they were not sure what the politicians who controlled the funds would believe. The group decided that it needed to publicize the unique features of its work, so that politicians, other funders, and the general public would recognize the niche that this collaborative initiative addressed.

Outcomes

By and large, participants' responses to their inventory ratings facilitated effective functioning of the collaborative group. A successful publicity campaign in the target neighborhood capitalized on the involvement of community and nonprofit organizations to increase knowledge of health and counseling services among residents. The campaign also improved the health department's reputation within the community. As hoped, these achievements showed members of the collaborating organizations that they could work together, thereby increasing their mutual trust and respect. Publicity efforts also succeeded in establishing the initiative as a unique and necessary part of health service provision in Tulip County. What's more, the group's interventions to improve social relationships among participants had the desired effect, creating a greater sense of camaraderie throughout the initiative.

As with any collaborative effort, however, the group suffered some setbacks. In particular, turnover among those involved led to the loss of a key participant, an employee of the health department who had been instrumental in establishing and maintaining open channels of communication. Because this individual had taken responsibility informally, participants at the retreat had been unaware of the boost her attention to communication had given to their ratings for that factor. With an average rating of 4.4, "Open and frequent communication" had simply been deemed a strength of the group, requiring little further thought. Thus, when the health department employee left the group, those that remained were unprepared for the ensuing disruption in their transfer of information. It was not until communication failures led to several minor problems that the group recognized its deficiency and intervened to correct it. This experience led the group to monitor more closely even those factors that appeared satisfactory at any given time.

CHAPTER 6

Summary and Conclusions

WE MENTIONED earlier that if our topic were gardening, the purpose of this publication would be to identify the critical elements necessary for growing a healthy, productive garden.

Chapters Two and Three might have identified factors such as levels of sunlight, water, air, or nutrients needed to produce a successful garden. Prospective gardeners could find out what "garden systems" require in order to thrive, and then apply their learning to the process of growing specific plants in specific sites. Some factors at those sites would come under the gardeners' complete control, but they would have little or no control over other factors.

As with gardens, successful collaborations require cultivation, and this book offers a guide to understanding the necessary ingredients for cultivating success.

In this closing chapter, let's review and summarize what we have discussed, and how the information can be used in your specific situation.

What We Have Learned

What have we learned from the preceding chapters that we might apply to our design, funding, and implementation of collaborative projects?

First, we learned what the current research tells us about the factors that produce success in collaborative efforts. Specifically, we concluded from the research that twenty factors appear to strongly influence the success of collaboration.[29]

---

[29] Research has also demonstrated the importance of very similar factors for "community building" efforts. See Mattessich and Monsey (1997) and Mattessich (2000).

We can have confidence in this conclusion because, in order to appear in our analysis, the studies we included in the development of this book had to offer clear and convincing findings. They had to relate to collaborative efforts that involved a nonprofit organization in partnership with one or more nonprofit, government, or business organizations. Furthermore, the research documenting the importance of the twenty factors consists of studies in which researchers monitored collaborative initiatives over time and identified the reasons why they worked (or didn't work). For each study, it is possible to link the success or failure of collaboration to the presence or absence of specific factors. These features of the studies included in this book ensure both their scientific credibility and their relevance.[30]

Second, we saw many examples that illustrated how the factors influenced success in specific initiatives. These examples came primarily from the research studies used to identify the factors. The examples informed us of the variety of ways that collaboration occurs and of the applicability of the results of research to many different types of activities (for example, health, community development, education, safety, and economic development).

Third, we saw how other practitioners and researchers have used the first edition of *Collaboration: What Makes It Work*. We noted the value of building systematically on what is known about collaborative success, rather than working in a vacuum.

Fourth, we reviewed the newest version of a tool, The Wilder Collaboration Factors Inventory, that can assist groups to see where they stand on the factors that influence success. We saw how some groups have used this tool to focus attention on their collaborative strengths and weaknesses and to help them decide whether and how to take corrective action. Groups have used the tool both in designing new collaborative projects as well as in reviewing efforts already in operation.

Using the Information

We know that the readers of this book include

- Nonprofit and government agency managers and staff whose work draws them into collaborative situations with other organizations.

- Funders, policy-makers, and other decision-makers who need to allocate resources based on the most cost-effective means to reach significant social goals.

- Others who work in, support, or advise collaborative groups.

---

[30] A complete description of the methodology for selecting studies and screening them to ensure quality appears in Appendix B. The description in Appendix B offers a "map" to other researchers who might want to delve more deeply into specific studies, or to inspect our findings to spot errors or inaccuracies, or to replicate our analysis at a later time with more research to see whether additional factors influence the success of collaboration. We promote this clear and open approach to methodology in order to foster self-discipline and high quality for our own work as well as to advance the overall state of collaboration research and practice.

We hope the book provides a theoretical understanding of the ingredients necessary for collaborative success. With a thorough grounding in the factors of successful collaboration, readers can decide how to apply that knowledge.

For example, the research clearly indicates that mutual respect, understanding, and trust (Factor 2A) must develop among collaborators in order for their project to succeed. There are a variety of ways, however, that collaborators can develop and maintain respect, understanding, and trust. For example, they can work on small, short-term projects as a way of coming to know and trust one another, before engaging in a major, long-term effort. They can host open houses, tours, or visits within one another's facilities, enabling people to meet one another and become more familiar and comfortable with the culture, operations, and physical locations of collaborating partners. They can simply spend time with one another—perhaps at parties or other social events. This familiarity and comfort will enhance mutual respect, understanding, and trust. Like a gardener striving to apply the principles of effective cultivation to a specific plot of land, collaborators must determine how to foster the success factors in the circumstances in which they find themselves.

Let's elaborate on how collaborating partners can apply what we know about collaborative success by discussing again the uses of this book that we talked about in Chapter One.

- **For general understanding.**

  Read the book to increase your knowledge of the success factors behind collaborative projects. You will then have a set of useful concepts in mind when you consider collaboration as an option for achieving your organization's goals.

  Some questions you might raise when you consider the option of collaborating with others to achieve a common goal:

  - Will it be possible to include all the factors necessary for success in your situation?

  - What will be the cost (time, money, other resources) of doing whatever it takes to make sure the success factors are included?

  - Do the expected benefits of the collaboration exceed the potential costs?

- In **specific situations:**

  Turn to the book when you need to plan or make a decision about a collaborative project you're involved in. The material in Chapters Two through Five can serve you in at least three ways:

  1. Use the set of success factors as a checklist, or complete The Wilder Collaboration Factors Inventory in Chapter Five, to determine if your group's plans or current activities include all necessary ingredients. If not, you can take steps to build in whatever the project lacks.

Questions you might want to ask include:

- How does a proposed project rate on each of the twenty factors? For example, is there a history of collaboration or cooperation in the community? Do members see collaboration as furthering their self-interest?

- If a proposed project rates low on a specific factor, is that a reason not to proceed, or can steps be taken to improve the rating?

- Has the planning of a proposed project built in mechanisms for both *developing* and *sustaining* the factors necessary for the success of the collaborative group?

2. Use the content of Chapter Three (especially the implications and illustrations sections) to expand your thinking about ways to help your collaborative project succeed, comparing your situation with others that might be similar.

   For example, in order for members of a collaborative group to share a stake in both the process and outcome of their work (Factor 3A), Chapter Three suggests that adequate time must be devoted to the process of developing "ownership" among all participants in a collaborative effort. How will you build in that time?

3. After you have a collaborative effort under way, return to the material in the book to ask, What should we be watching out for? Are there changes we need to make in midcourse?

   For example, you might find that you and the other collaborating partners did a good job building flexibility (Factor 3C) into your collaboration at the start. However, over time, members have slowly become more rigid, and this rigidity has decreased your efficiency, if not your overall likelihood of success.

4. Pay special attention to the new factor identified in this edition: appropriate pace of development (Factor 3F). Are you moving too quickly or too slowly? Do you need to plan a gradual increase in relationships, use of resources, intensity of effort, or complexity of tasks, in order to increase the likelihood of success?

The Importance of the Factors for Your Situation

What is the proper "mix" of factors? Are some more important and some less important? Can a project succeed if it has most, but not all, of the factors?

Unfortunately, no simple answers exist for these questions. (In fact, they are some of the questions that we feel merit research.)

Recall from Chapter Two that the factor identified by the largest number of studies had to do with mutual respect, understanding, and trust. This would imply that interpersonal and psychological attributes of the partners within a collaborative group have more importance than anything else when it comes to helping a collaborative initiative to succeed. Therefore, potential collaborators might conclude they should concentrate most heavily on building the right attitudes and spirit among partners in order to increase their chances for success.

On the other hand, quite frankly, a greater number of studies identifying a factor could just mean that the factor was better known to the researchers, or easier to measure, so they focused on it to see if it was important. In the first edition of this book, the largest number of studies identified a different factor, appropriate cross section of members.

Since we lack sufficiently precise research findings to assert the relative importance of one factor over another, it is probably best to recall our garden analogy. Sunlight is a factor necessary for a garden. If sunlight is totally absent, the garden will not grow at all. However, if sunlight is present to some degree, the garden will still produce results.

As with the garden, it's likely that without certain ingredients, collaboration is impossible. Nonetheless, some benefits of collaboration can be achieved even if the success factors aren't present in ideal amounts. For example, if no trust exists among collaborators, the collaborative effort has about as much chance of succeeding as a garden without any sunlight. However, if partners at least minimally trust each other, they can probably reach many of their goals, even if they can't achieve as much as they would in a situation of very great trust. Keep in mind, too, that many factors are interrelated—building one may strengthen another.

Prudent collaborators will devote attention to all the factors, to ensure that their collaborative initiatives have the greatest likelihood of success.

A Word about the Future

We look forward to the next decades of collaboration practice and research. The level of complexity and interdependence of our modern world means that no community or society exists in isolation. Events in a different hemisphere can have an impact on local economies, local customs, and local institutions that is as strong as the impact from events just a short distance away. In addition, modern communication technology ties us together more effectively than ever before. People can link up with one another for joint efforts across the miles almost as easily as if they sat in the same room.

As a consequence of world trends, people will inevitably see joint efforts as a necessity for addressing economic, social, environmental, legal, and other issues that transcend community and national boundaries. They will realize that the fields of art, education, literature, and indeed all of culture will advance in the most exciting and productive ways through joint efforts among practitioners. Whether at the level of nation-states or at the grassroots level of communities coexisting within a city, town, or region, people will increasingly recognize the importance of working jointly with others to achieve common goals.

Within such an interdependent world, collaboration will likely become a more important tool. It won't be appropriate in all situations for all tasks. Sometimes, other types of joint efforts will have greater effectiveness or efficiency. However, collaboration will remain an important instrument to use when appropriate.

In all forms of human knowledge, we learn through an ongoing process in which we repeat the cycle of planning, doing, and reflecting. Knowledge about collaboration has developed in that way, and will continue to do so. Practitioners base their activities on the best knowledge as of a certain time and then learn from their experience, making revisions in their plans the next time they try something. Researchers such as ourselves monitor and codify the learning and transmit it to others for their use.

We see this book as one step in the progression of knowledge about collaboration. We know a great deal, yet much remains to be learned. The future experiences of those who practice collaboration will produce new knowledge that will help all of us succeed in our partnership initiatives to produce better communities and a better world!

Appendices

APPENDIX A

Definition of Collaboration

Our working definition of collaboration is:

> ***Collaboration*** *is a mutually beneficial and well-defined relationship entered into by two or more organizations to achieve common goals.*
>
> *The relationship includes a commitment to mutual relationships and goals; a jointly developed structure and shared responsibility; mutual authority and accountability for success; and sharing of resources and rewards.*[31]

Defining collaboration is made complex by ambiguities in practical usage and scholarly disagreement about the term. In practical use, "collaboration" is commonly interchanged with "cooperation" and "coordination." In most scholarly writing, however, cooperation, coordination, and collaboration have distinct meanings.

---

[31] We are indebted to author and collaboration consultant Michael Winer for his work on this definition. He combined the work of several experts to draft both the definition and the accompanying description of how collaboration differs from coordination and cooperation.

Cooperation is characterized by informal relationships that exist without any commonly defined mission, structure, or planning effort. Information is shared as needed, and authority is retained by each organization so there is virtually no risk. Resources are separate as are rewards.

Coordination is characterized by more formal relationships and an understanding of compatible missions. Some planning and division of roles are required, and communication channels are established. Authority still rests with the individual organizations, but there is some increased risk to all participants. Resources are available to participants and rewards are mutually acknowledged.

Collaboration connotes a more durable and pervasive relationship. Collaborations bring previously separated organizations into a new structure with full commitment to a common mission. Such relationships require comprehensive planning and well-defined communication channels operating on many levels. Authority is determined by the collaborative structure. Risk is much greater because each member of the collaboration contributes its own resources and reputation. Resources are pooled or jointly secured, and the products are shared.

The table on page 61 compares cooperation, coordination, and collaboration.

Cooperation, Coordination, and Collaboration
A Table Describing the Elements of Each [32]

Essential Elements	Cooperation	Coordination	Collaboration
Vision and Relationships	• Basis for cooperation is usually between individuals but may be mandated by a third party	• Individual relationships are supported by the organizations they represent	• Commitment of the organizations and their leaders is fully behind their representatives
	• Organizational missions and goals are not taken into account	• Missions and goals of the individual organizations are reviewed for compatibility	• Common, new mission and goals are created
	• Interaction is on an as needed basis, may last indefinitely	• Interaction is usually around one specific project or task of definable length	• One or more projects are undertaken for longer-term results
Structure, Responsibilities, Communication	• Relationships are informal; each organization functions separately	• Organizations involved take on needed roles, but function relatively independently of each other	• New organizational structure and/or clearly defined and interrelated roles that constitute a formal division of labor are created
	• No joint planning is required	• Some project-specific planning is required	• More comprehensive planning is required that includes developing joint strategies and measuring success in terms of impact on the needs of those served
	• Information is conveyed as needed	• Communication roles are established and definite channels are created for interaction	• Beyond communication roles and channels for interaction, many "levels" of communication are created as clear information is a keystone of success
Authority and Accountability	• Authority rests solely with individual organizations	• Authority rests with the individual organizations, but there is coordination among participants	• Authority is determined by the collaboration to balance ownership by the individual organizations with expediency to accomplish purpose
	• Leadership is unilateral and control is central	• Some sharing of leadership and control	• Leadership is dispersed, and control is shared and mutual
	• All authority and accountability rests with the individual organization which acts independently	• There is some shared risk, but most of the authority and accountability falls to the individual organizations	• Equal risk is shared by all organizations in the collaboration
Resources and Rewards	• Resources (staff time, dollars, and capabilities) are separate, serving the individual organization's needs	• Resources are acknowledged and can be made available to others for a specific project	• Resources are pooled or jointly secured for a longer-term effort that is managed by the collaborative structure
		• Rewards are mutually acknowledged	• Organizations share in the products; more is accomplished jointly than could have been individually

[32] Adapted from the works of Martin Blank, Sharon Kagan, Atelia Melaville, and Karen Ray.

Methodology

The review and summary of research related to collaboration had three major stages:

1. Identification and Assessment of Research Studies
2. Systematic Codification of Findings from Each Study
3. Synthesis of Findings from Individual Studies

These stages structured the research process for both editions of this publication. With some exceptions, the screening and review procedures were the same for the revision as they were for the original work. These procedures are described in detail below. Where the methodology differed between the two phases, all changes are noted.

1. Identification and Assessment of Research Studies

A. Formulation of a Precise Research Question

In order to set both goals and parameters for the research review, a precise research question was required. This question was formulated as

"What factors influence the success of collaborative efforts among organizations in the human services, government, and other nonprofit fields?"

This question oriented the work in several ways. It established that the research to be included in the review (the meta-analysis) must

- Focus on collaboration.
- Have relevance for the collaboration that occurs among human services, government, and other nonprofit organizations.[33]

---

[33] Note that this requirement does not mean that all studies had to involve organizations in these fields, only that the results had to be relevant to these organizations. In point of fact, most, but not all, of the studies reviewed in this report involved human services, government, or other nonprofit organizations.

- Relate to the success of a collaborative endeavor (measured in terms of outcomes)—not merely to the reasons for collaboration, the process, or other features.

B. Collection of Potentially Relevant Studies

Research staff then searched for and collected all pieces of work that were reported to be "collaboration research." The following search techniques were used:

- Computerized bibliographic searches in the areas of social science, health, education, and public affairs
- Personal inquiries to researchers known for their interest in the topic, to obtain both their work and references to the work of others
- Tracking down (in a snowball fashion) bibliographic references appearing in materials as they were gathered
- For this revision, a search of the Internet for relevant references

These activities led to the acquisition of references to 133 studies in 1992, and an additional 281 studies in 2000.

C. Development of Acceptance Criteria

Meta-analytic research reviews require the establishment of criteria by which every potential study for inclusion in the final analysis is determined to be acceptable or unacceptable.

For the collaboration research review, research staff established that a study had to meet the following criteria for inclusion in the review:

1. The study must address the major research question (as described above).

2. The joint organizational effort analyzed by the study must meet the definition of "collaboration" developed for this research project. That is, it must truly be a *collaborative group,* not merely a loose cooperative or coordinated arrangement.[34]

3. The study must address the topic of success of the collaborative group.

4. The study report must include some sort of specific, empirical observations. It could not merely represent the "thoughts" of an expert; nor could it merely contain generalizations based on "broad experience."

5. The study must be sufficiently translated into English, if it was not originally reported in English.

---

[34] See Appendix A for the definition of collaboration and its differences from other forms of joint efforts.

D. Initial Screening of Studies

Brief information was obtained for as many of the potentially relevant studies as possible. This included abstracts and summaries that enabled the research staff to assess the probable worth of a particular study, based on a very liberal application of the acceptance criteria listed above. For each research study estimated to have probable worth, research staff attempted to obtain a complete report from the study. These reports came in the form of journal articles, formally published reports, and informally published (or typically unpublished) reports.

This screening reduced the number of potential studies to sixty-two in 1992; in 2000, seventy-five new studies remained after the screening.[35]

E. Critical Assessment of Studies

For each of the complete studies in hand, researchers made a critical assessment of whether the study met the acceptance criteria for inclusion in the research review. At this point, the criteria were very strictly applied. Studies were dropped because they did not address the major research question adequately; the projects did not meet our definition of collaboration; they did not include empirical observations; or they did not address the topic of success.

This assessment reduced the number of studies to eighteen in 1992 and twenty-two in 2000, for a total of forty valid and relevant studies.

2. Systematic Codification of Findings from Each Study

A. Development of a Methodology

The central research question asked for the identification of factors that influence the success of collaboration. A typical meta-analysis would pool all the empirical studies that analyzed the relationship between a specific factor and collaborative success. Based on this pooling, a result would emerge, identifying the importance, if any, of the factor.[36]

The problem with research on collaboration is that virtually every study employs only a case study methodology, not detailed empirical methods. Case studies are not amenable to the pooling of quantifiable data.

Therefore, we needed to develop a way to:

- Identify the success factors that each case study demonstrated.

- Blend the results from all the studies included in this analysis into one set of factors.

---

[35] In 1992, thirty-six studies were dropped from consideration because they failed to meet the acceptance criteria; thirty-five were dropped because complete study reports simply could not be obtained. In 2000, 156 studies were dropped because they did not meet the acceptance criteria, and fifty were dropped because complete reports could not be obtained.

[36] For good overviews of the process of meta-analysis, see: Rosenthal (1991), Light and Pillemer (1984). For a discussion of some of the challenges facing meta-analysis, see Iyengar (1991).

B. Identification of Factors

The primary methodological rules developed for culling success factors from case studies were that:

1. The case study must include a statement by the case researcher that a particular factor is something that influenced the success of the collaborative group that was studied.

2. It must be possible for an outside observer (in this case, a Wilder Research Center researcher) to link the statement by the case researcher about the factor directly to evidence in the case study of its effect upon success.

Even within a review of empirical research studies, this can be a difficult task. In working with case studies, it becomes a monumental challenge.[37]

To accomplish this task, a Wilder Research Center researcher carefully reviewed each study, identifying factors that were stated in the study to influence success and that could be linked to study evidence.

C. Validation of Factors

In 1992, a second Wilder Research Center researcher independently reviewed each of the case studies and critically examined the evidence related to each factor identified by the first researcher to validate that it met the two criteria listed in (A). In 2000, the researchers jointly discussed each of the factors identified by the first researcher.

The fact that the researchers, in 2000, built upon the initial meta-analysis conducted for the first edition of *Collaboration: What Makes It Work* has both advantages and disadvantages. The advantages are that some effort is channeled directly into determining whether the initial nineteen factors in the first edition withstand further scrutiny and that the new work deliberately uses the initial research base as a foundation for expansion. The major disadvantage is that the results of the first edition impose a frame of reference upon later researchers who might miss some new insights because their perspective is limited.[38]

---

[37] Rosenthal (1991, p. 13) insightfully observes, for example, that by "research results," we "do not mean the conclusion drawn by the investigator, since that is often only vaguely related to the actual results. The metamorphosis that sometimes occurs between the results section and the discussion section is itself a topic worthy of detailed consideration. For now, it is enough to note that a fairly ambiguous result often becomes quite smooth and rounded in the discussion section, so that reviewers who dwell too much on the discussion and too little on the results can be quite misled as to what actually was found."

[38] As Chalmers (1999, p. 17) points out, the attempt to capture "the facts" becomes difficult due to the "extent to which perceptions are influenced by the background and expectations of the observer," as well as "the extent to which judgments about the truth of observation statements depend on what is already known or assumed, thus rendering the observable facts as fallible as the presuppositions underlying them." Having factors from the first edition in place creates the potential for perceptual bias within the research for the second edition. However, the research was pursued with careful attention to rules established for the study, and this appendix provides a full explication of the study methods to enable others to conduct the same inquiry. In this way, the research gains the greatest possible validity. Both the findings and the methods for producing the findings are available for scrutiny by all who are interested. Others can refine the methods and improve upon these findings.

3. Synthesis of Findings from Individual Studies

A. Determining the List of Factors

The list of factors from individual studies was examined. In some cases, the wording of factors in two or more studies was identical; and they could easily be counted as the same. In other cases, the wording differed slightly. In these cases, two researchers looked closely at the factors and their associated case studies and decided whether the factors were the same.

In 1992, this process led to the identification of nineteen factors from the combined findings of eighteen studies.[39] In 2000, an additional twenty-two studies provided confirmation of the original nineteen factors and led to the identification of one new factor. So, in total, this report describes twenty success factors based on the findings of forty valid and relevant studies.

B. Tallying the Importance of Factors

For the final list of factors, the number of studies that cite each factor was tallied. The tallies in the current edition include tallies from the first and second rounds of research. The result provides a rough estimate of the importance of a factor or its weight in influencing collaborative success. Case study results cannot provide quantified estimates beyond this, future research on collaboration could do so (if it becomes more quantitative).

C. Putting the Factors into Categories

For ease of presentation, discussion, and use, the factors in both editions appear in six categories. There is no research significance to the category groupings or to their names. If users of the book feel that a different grouping is appropriate, they can develop new categories without compromising the basic meta-analytic work.

---

[39] All factors are stated in the "positive," even though studies may have stated their "negative" dimension or indicated that the lack of a factor produced failure.

Collaboration Experts Interviewed

FOR BOTH editions of this report, a number of experts in the field of collaboration participated in interviews to provide us with leads, suggestions, and advice. These experts directed us to relevant research studies, offered valuable feedback, and were an essential source of up-to-date information from the field. Their names are listed below.

1992 Edition

Bryan Barry
Wilder Foundation
Services to Organizations

Ruth Belzer
The Harris Foundation

Renee Berger
Director of Team Works

Martin Blank
Senior Associate
The Institute for Educational
    Leadership, Inc.

Dave Brown
Institute for Development Research

Cheryle Casciani
Annie E. Casey Foundation

Louis Delgado
John and Katherine T. MacArthur
    Foundation

D. D. (David) Dill
University of North Carolina-Chapel Hill

Sheri Dodd
Joining Forces

Barbara Gray
Penn State University
College of Business Administration
Department of Management and
    Organization

Dr. Gloria Harbin
University of North Carolina-Chapel Hill
Carolina Institute for Child
    and Family Policy

Shirley Hord
Southwest Educational
    Development Lab

John Johnson
Changemaking Systems
Burnsville, MN

Sharon L. Kagan
Bush Center for Child
    Development and Social Policy

Karen Ray
Karen Ray Associates
Minnetonka, MN

Cheryl Rogers
Senior Research Associate
Center for the Study of Social Policy

Linda Silver
Wilder Foundation
Community Care Resources

Gene Urbain
Wilder Foundation
Parent Outreach Project

2001 Edition

Bryan Barry
Wilder Foundation
Wilder Center for Communities

Martin Blank
Senior Associate
The Institute for Educational
    Leadership, Inc.

Barbara Gray
Penn State University
College of Business Administration
Department of Management and
    Organization

Chris Huxham
Strathclyde Graduate Business School

Sharon L. Kagan
Bush Center for Child Development
    and Social Policy

Carol Lukas
Wilder Foundation
Wilder Center for Communities

Elizabeth Mulroy
University of Maryland
School of Social Work

APPENDIX D

Author/Factor Matrix

THE FOLLOWING CHART cross-classifies each factor with each study that identified it. Studies are listed alphabetically by authors' names. Full citations appear in the bibliography.

	Abbott et al. 95	Agranoff and Lindsay 83	Alaszewski and Harrison 88	Auluck and Iles 91	Austin 00	Bierly 88	Block et al. 99	Campbell et al. 99	Chrislip and Larson 94	Coe 88	Davidson 76	Gray 95/Gray 96[40]
1. Factors Related to the Environment												
A. History of collaboration or cooperation in the community	•				•	•		•			•	
B. Collaborative group seen as a legitimate leader in the community										•		
C. Favorable political and social climate												
2. Factors Related to Membership Characteristics												
A. Mutual respect, understanding, and trust	•	•		•	•	•	•	•	•	•		•
B. Appropriate cross section of members		•					•	•		•		•
C. Members see collaboration as in their self-interest	•	•			•			•	•		•	
D. Ability to compromise		•						•		•		
3. Factors Related to Process/Structure												
A. Members share a stake in both process and outcome		•							•	•		•
B. Multiple layers of participation	•	•	•		•					•		•
C. Flexibility		•			•			•				
D. Development of clear roles and policy guidelines							•	•		•	•	
E. Adaptability		•										
F. Appropriate pace of development					•				•		•	
4. Factors Related to Communication												
A. Open and frequent communication.		•	•	•	•	•				•		
B. Established informal relationships and communication links	•					•	•		•			
5. Factors Related to Purpose												
A. Concrete, attainable goals and objectives		•						•	•	•		
B. Shared vision						•			•	•		
C. Unique purpose										•		
6. Factors Related to Resources												
A. Sufficient funds, staff, materials, and time	•	•	•				•				•	
B. Skilled leadership							•		•	•	•	

---

[40] Gray (1996) describes two cases of collaboration. Sharfman et al. (1991) described one of the same cases treated in Gray (1996). For that particular case, Sharfman et al. identified four factors, but Gray only identified two. To avoid duplication of factors, we selected the Sharfman et al. treatment of that case, and all four of the factors are referenced in the Sharfman et al. column of this table. The second case described in Gray (1996) is also described in Gray (1995). The Gray 95/Gray 96 column of this table provides a list of all the factors identified in this second case.

Column headings (left to right):

1. Hackstaff-Goldis and House 90
2. Harbert et al. 97
3. Harbin et al. 91
4. Harrison et al. 90
5. Hodson et al. 76
6. Holman and Arcus 87
7. Horwitch and Prahalad 81
8. Isles and Auluck 90
9. Kagan et al. 90
10. Lennett and Colten 99
11. Lukas and Weiss 95
12. Mayfield and Lucas 00
13. McCann and Gray 86
14. Means et al. 91
15. Mulroy 97
16. Pitt 98
17. Reilly and Petersen 97
18. Rist et al. 80[41]
19. Rogers et al. 96
20. Rubin 98
21. Sharfman et al. 91
22. Subramanian et al. 94
23. Tapper et al. 97
24. Trubowitz and Longo 97
25. Urban and Bennett 99
26. Wiewel and Guerrero 97
27. Wiewel and Lieber 98[42]
28. Yon et al. 93

[41] The success factors described in this report include only those that are identified by at least three studies. When the first edition was published, "appropriate pace of development" had been identified as a success factor by Rist and his colleagues, but was not included in the matrix for lack of corroboration. Since that time, several other studies have confirmed the importance of good timing in effective collaborative work.

[42] Wiewel and Lieber (1998), Wiewel and Guerrero (1997), and Mayfield and Lucas (2000) are studies of the University of Illinois at Chicago Neighborhoods Initiative (UICNI). Broadly conceived, the UICNI is a collaboration between the university and its surrounding communities. This umbrella collaboration subsumes a number of smaller, ongoing collaborations between the university and individual community organizations. The Mayfield and Lucas and Wiewel and Guerrero studies each examined a specific project within the UICNI, while the Wiewel and Lieber study drew conclusions from the initiative as a whole. It is therefore likely that Wiewel and Lieber's analysis is based, at least in part, on cases of collaboration that appear in the other UICNI studies. In order to avoid duplication, we excluded from the matrix three factors identified by Wiewel and Lieber that were also identified by either Mayfield and Lucas or Wiewel and Guerrero.

Bibliography

Abbott, Beverly, Pat Jordan, and Niaz Murtaza
   1995   "Interagency Collaboration for Children's Mental Health Services: The San Mateo County Model for Managed Care." *Administration and Policy in Mental Health* 22(3): 301–313.

Agranoff, Robert and Valerie Lindsay
   1983   "Intergovernmental Management: Perspectives from Human Services Problem Solving at the Local Level." *Public Administration Review* May/June: 227–237.

Alaszewski, Andy and Larry Harrison
   1988   "Literature Review: Collaboration and Co-ordination Between Welfare Agencies." *British Journal of Social Work* 18: 635–647.

Altman, Lawrence
   1990   "New Method of Analyzing Health Data Stirs Debate." *New York Times,* August 21, 1990, p. B5.

Aronstein, David M. and Michael A. Connolly
   1999   "Access to Life-Saving Medicine: A Collaboration Between a Not-For-Profit HIV Clinical Research Agency, a State Public Health Department, and For-Profit Pharmaceutical Companies." In *Crossing the Borders: Collaboration and Competition Among Nonprofits, Business and Government.* Washington, D.C.: Independent Sector.

Ashman, Darcy
   2000   "Promoting Corporate Citizenship in the Global South: Towards a Model of Empowered Civil Society Collaboration with Business." *IDR Reports* 16(3).

Auluck, Randhir and Paul Iles
  1991   "The Referral Process: A Study of Working Relationships Between Ante-natal Clinic Nursing Staff and Hospital Social Workers and Their Impact on Asian Women." *British Journal of Social Work* 21: 41–61.

Austin, James E.
  2000   *The Collaboration Challenge: How Nonprofits and Businesses Succeed Through Strategic Alliances.* San Francisco: Jossey-Bass.

Bierly, Eugene W.
  1988   "The World Climate Program: Collaboration and Communication on a Global Scale." *The Annals* 495: 106–116.

Block, Carolyn Rebecca, Barbara Engel, Sara M. Naureckas, and Kim A. Riordan
  1999   "The Chicago Women's Health Risk Study." *Violence Against Women* 5(10): 1158–1177.

Campbell, Jacquelyn C., Jacqueline Dienemann, Joan Kub, Terri Wurmser, and Ellyn Loy
  1999   "Collaboration as a Partnership." *Violence Against Women* 5(10): 1140–1157.

Center for Ocean Sciences Education Excellence
  2000   "Report of a Workshop Sponsored by the National Science Foundation, in Cooperation with the University of Southern Mississippi, Institute of Marine Sciences." Seattle, WA: University of Washington.

Center for the Study of Social Policy
  1991   "The New Futures Initiative: A Mid-Point Review." Washington, D.C.: Center for the Study of Social Policy.

Chalmers, Alan F.
  1999   *What Is This Thing Called Science?* Buckingham, England: Open University Press.

Chrislip, David D. and Carl E. Larson
  1994   *Collaborative Leadership: How Citizens and Civic Leaders Can Make a Difference.* San Francisco: Jossey-Bass.

Coe, Barbara
  1988   "Open Focus: Implementing Projects in Multi-Organizational Settings." *International Journal of Public Administration* 11(4): 503–526.

Cook, Thomas D., Harris Cooper, David S. Cordray, Heidi Hartmann, Larry V. Hedges, Richard J. Light, Thomas A. Louis, and Frederick Mosteller
  1992   *Meta-Analysis for Exploration.* New York: Russell Sage Foundation.

Cooper, Harris and Larry V. Hedges (Eds.)
  1994   *The Handbook of Research Synthesis.* New York: Russell Sage Foundation.

Davidson, Stephen
   1976   "Planning and Coordination of Social Services in Multiorganizational Contexts." *Social Service Review* 50: 117–137.

Dayton, Carol, Georgia J. Anetzberger, and Doris Matthey
   1997   "A Model for Service Coordination Between Mental Health and Adult Protective Services." *Journal of Mental Health and Aging* 3(3): 295–308.

Fischer, Lucy Rose and Kay Schaffer
   1992   *Older Volunteers: A Guide to Research and Practice.* Newbury Park, CA: Sage Publications.

Gans, S.P. and G.T. Horton
   1975   *"Integration of Human Services."* New York: Praeger.

Gozali-Lee, Edith
   1999   "Family Involvement to Promote Student Achievement." Saint Paul, MN: Wilder Research Center.

Gray, Barbara
   1989   *Collaborating.* San Francisco: Jossey-Bass.

Gray, Barbara
   1995   "Obstacles to Success in Educational Collaborations." In Leo C. Rigsby, Maynard C. Reynolds, and Margaret C. Wang (Eds.), *School-Community Connections: Exploring Issues for Research and Practice* (pp. 71–99). San Francisco: Jossey-Bass.

Gray, Barbara
   1996   "Cross-Sectoral Partners: Collaborative Alliances among Business, Government and Communities." In Chris Huxham (Ed.), *Creating Collaborative Advantage* (pp. 57–79). London: Sage.

Hackstaff-Goldis, Lynn and Susan T. House
   1990   "Development of a Collaborative Geriatric Program Between the Legal System and a Social Work-Directed Program of a Community Hospital." *Social Work in Health Care* 14(3): 1–16.

Harbert, Anita S., Daniel Finnegan, and Nancy Tyler
   1997   "Collaboration: A Study of a Children's Initiative." *Administration in Social Work* 21(3–4): 83-107.

Harbin, Gloria, Jane Eckland, James Gallagher, Richard Clifford, and Patricia Place
   1991   "Policy Development for P.L. 99–457, Part H: Initial Findings from Six Case Studies." Carolina Institute for Child and Family Policy, University of North Carolina, Chapel Hill, NC.

Harrison, Patrick J., Eleanor W. Lynch, Kendra Rosander, and William Borton
1990   "Determining Success in Interagency Collaboration: An Evaluation of Processes and Behaviors." *Infants and Young Children* 3(1): 69–78.

Himmelman, Arthur
1990   "Community-Based Collaborations: Working Together for a Change." *Northwest Report* November 1990, p. 26.

Hodson, Norma, Mary Ann Armour, and John Touliatos
1976   "Project Uplift: A Coordinated Youth Services System." *The Family Coordinator* 25 (3): 255–260.

Holman, Nicole and Margaret Arcus
1987   "Helping Adolescent Mothers and Their Children: An Integrated Multi-Agency Approach." *Family Relations* 36(2): 119–123.

Horwitch, Mel and C.K. Prahalad
1981   "Managing Multi-Organization Enterprises: The Emerging Strategic Frontier." *Sloan Management Review* 22(2): 3–16.

Huxham, Chris
1996   *Creating Collaborative Advantage*. London: Sage.

Huxham, Chris and Siv Vangen
1996   "Working Together: Key Themes in the Management of Relationships Between Public and Non-Profit Organizations." *International Journal of Public Sector Management* 9(7): 5–17.

Huxham, Chris and Siv Vangen
2000   "Ambiguity, Complexity and Dynamics in the Membership of Collaboration." *Human Relations* 53(6): 771–806.

Isles, Paul and Randhir Auluck
1990   "Team Building, Inter-agency Team Development and Social Work Practice." *British Journal of Social Work* 20: 165–178.

Iyengar, Satish
1991   "Much Ado About Meta-Analysis." *Chance: New Directions for Statistics and Computing* 4(1): 33–40.

Kagan, Sharon L.
1991   *United We Stand: Collaboration for Child Care and Early Education Services*. New York: Teachers College Press.

Kagan, Sharon L., Ann Marie Rivera, and Faith Lamb Parker
1990   "Collaboration in Practice: Reshaping Services for Young Children and Their Families." The Bush Center in Child Development and Social Policy, Yale University.

Karasoff, Patricia
1998   "Collaborative Partnerships: A Review of the Literature." San Francisco State University.

Kerka, Sandra
1997   "Developing Collaborative Partnerships." Washington, D.C.: U.S. Department of Education.

Lennett, Judith and Mary Ellen Colten
1999   "A Winning Alliance: Collaboration of Advocates and Researchers on the Massachusetts Mothers Survey." *Violence Against Women* 5(10): 1118–1139.

Light, Richard J. and David B. Pillemer
1984   *Summing Up: The Science of Reviewing Research.* Cambridge, MA: Harvard University Press.

Loch, Heather, Daniel P. Mueller, and Edith Gozali-Lee
1997   "Key Issues in the Implementation of School Linked Services." Saint Paul, MN: Wilder Research Center.

Lukas, Carol VanDeusen and Heather B. Weiss
1995   "Evaluation of the Head Start/Community Health Center Collaboration: A Final Report to the Prudential Foundation." Harvard Family Research Project, Cambridge, MA.

Mattessich, Paul W.
2000   "Characteristics of Successful Community Building and Collaborative Efforts." In Sandra Schruijer (Ed.), *Multi-Organizational Partnerships and Cooperative Strategy.* Tilburg, Netherlands: University of Tilburg Press.

Mattessich, Paul W. and Barbara R. Monsey
1992   *Collaboration: What Makes It Work.* Saint Paul, MN: Fieldstone Alliance.

Mattessich, Paul W. and Barbara R. Monsey
1997   *Community Building: What Makes It Work.* Saint Paul, MN: Fieldstone Alliance.

Mayfield, Loomis and Edgar P. Lucas
2000   "Mutual Awareness, Mutual Respect: The Community and the University Interact." *Cityscape* 5(1): 173–184.

McCann, Joseph E. and Barbara Gray
1986   "Power and Collaboration in Human Service Domains." *International Journal of Sociology and Social Policy* 6(3): 58–67.

The McKnight Foundation
1991   *The Aid to Families in Poverty Program.* Minneapolis, MN: The McKnight Foundation.

Means, Robin, Lyn Harrison, Syd Jeffers, and Randall Smith
1991   "Co-Ordination, Collaboration and Health Promotion: Lessons and Issues from an Alcohol/Education Programme." *Health Promotion International* 6(1) :31-39.

Melaville, Atelia with Martin J. Blank
1991   "What It Takes: Structuring Interagency Partnerships to Connect Children and Families with Comprehensive Services." Washington, D.C.: Education and Human Services Consortium.

Monsey, Barbara, Greg Owen, Carol Zierman, Laura Lambert, and Vincent Hyman
1995   *What Works in Preventing Rural Violence: Strategies, Risk Factors, and Assessment Tools.* Saint Paul, MN: Fieldstone Alliance.

Morse, Suzanne W.
1996   *Building Collaborative Communities.* Charlottesville, VA: Pew Partnership for Civic Change.

Mueller, Daniel P.
1997   "Characteristics of Successful Urban Elementary Schools." Saint Paul, MN: Wilder Research Center.

Mueller, Daniel P. and Paul Higgins
1988   *Funders' Guide Manual: A Guide to Prevention Programs in Human Services.* Saint Paul, MN: Wilder Foundation.

Mulroy, Elizabeth A.
1997   "Building a Neighborhood Network: Interorganizational Collaboration to Prevent Child Abuse and Neglect." *Social Work* 42(3): 255–264.

O'Donnell, Julie, James Ferreira, Ralph Hurtado, Ellen Ames, Richard E. Floyd, Jr., and Lottie M. Sebren
1998   "Partners for Change: Community Residents and Agencies." *Journal of Sociology and Social Welfare* 25(1): 133–151.

Pitt, Jessica
1998   *Community-Based Collaboratives: A Study of Interorganizational Cooperation at the Neighborhood Level.* Washington, D.C.: Aspen Institute.

Potapchuk, William R. and Jarle P. Crocker
1999   "Exploring the Elements of Civic Capital." *National Civic Review* 88(3): 175–201.

Reilly, Thom and Nancy Petersen
1997   "Nevada's University-State Partnership: A Comprehensive Alliance for Improved Services to Children and Families." *Public Welfare* 55(2): 21–28.

Rist, Ray C., Mary Agnes Hamilton, Wilfred B. Holloway, Steven D. Johnson, and
    Heather E. Wiltberger
    1980   "Collaboration and Community." Interim Report #4, Youthwork National
            Policy Study, Cornell University, Ithaca, NY.

Rogers, Kristen, Jill Duerr Berrick, and Richard P. Barth
    1996   "Collaboration and Community Empowerment for Primary Prevention."
            Child Welfare Research Center, University of California, Berkeley, CA.

Rosenthal, Robert
    1991   *Meta-Analytic Procedures for Social Research.* Newbury Park, CA: Sage.

Rubin, Victor
    1998   "The Roles of Universities in Community-Building Initiatives." *Journal of
            Planning Education and Research* 17: 302–311.

Sharfman, Mark P., Barbara Gray, and Aimin Yan
    1991   "The Context of Interorganizational Collaboration in the Garment Industry:
            An Institutional Perspective." *Special Issue on Collaboration in The Jour-
            nal of Applied Behavior Science.*

Subramanian, Karen, Elizabeth J. Siegel, and Christiane Garcia
    1994   "Case Study of an Agency-University Research Partnership Between a
            School of Social Work and a Medical Center." *Journal of Social Service
            Research* 19(3/4): 145–161.

Sussman, Tara
    2000   "Interagency Collaboration and Welfare Reform." Washington, D.C.: Wel-
            fare Information Network.

Tapper, Donna, Paula Kleinman, and Mary Nakashian
    1997   "An Interagency Collaboration Strategy for Linking Schools with Social
            and Criminal Justice Services." *Social Work in Education* 19(3): 176–188.

Trubowitz, Sidney and Paul Longo
    1997   *How It Works: Inside a School-College Collaboration.* New York: Teachers
            College Press.

Urban, Beverly Younger and Larry W. Bennett
    1999   "When the Community Punches a Time Clock." *Violence Against Women*
            5(10): 1178–1193.

Van de Ven, Andrew
    1976   "On the Nature, Formation, and Maintenance of Relations Among Organi-
            zations." *Academy of Management Review* 4: 24–36.

Wachter, K. W. and M. L. Straf (Eds.)
    1990   *The Future of Meta-Analysis.* New York: Russell Sage Foundation.

Walls, Wendell J.
   2000   *Anatomy of a Collaboration: An Act of Servant Leadership.* Indianapolis, IN: Greenleaf Center for Servant-Leadership.

Wiewel, Wim and Ismael Guerrero
   1997   "Long-term Collaboration—Building Relationships and Achieving Results through a Neighborhoods Initiative Program: The Resurrection Project." *Metropolitan Universities* 8(3): 123–134.

Wiewel, Wim and Michael Lieber
   1998   "Goal Achievement, Relationship Building, and Incrementalism: The Challenges of University-Community Partnerships." *Journal of Planning Education and Research* 17: 291–301.

Wilson, Betsy
   2000   "The Lone Ranger Is Dead—Success Today Demands Collaboration." Chicago, IL: Association of College and Resource Libraries.

Yon, Maria Grace, Roslyn Arlin Mickelson, and Iris Carlton-LaNey
   1993   "A Child's Place: Developing Interagency Collaboration on Behalf of Homeless Children." *Education and Urban Society* 25(4): 410–423.

Get the most complete picture of how your collaboration is doing

Buy copies of the inventory so each collaboration member can give their input

You can buy and distribute individual copies of the inventory to a small group of leaders in the collaborative, during a general meeting, or via mail to all members for the most complete picture of how your collaboration is doing. You can tally your score manually or online at www.FieldstoneAlliance.org.

Groups that are considering collaboration can use the inventory to see if they have what they need to succeed. They can then act quickly to shore up weaknesses and capitalize on strengths—before formalizing the collaboration, or in its early stages.

Established collaborations can use it to troubleshoot problems, demonstrate successes to funders, and uncover differences in how participating organizations perceive the collaboration.

Consultants to collaborations can use the tool to help the collaboration assess itself and to intervene for the most effective results.

The inventory includes complete instructions for administering, scoring, and interpreting the results, plus a definition of collaboration and descriptions of the twenty success factors.

See ordering information for how to order.

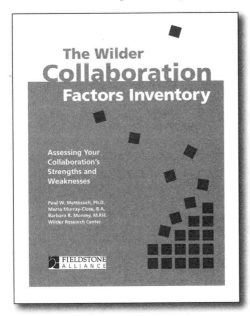

More results-oriented books from Fieldstone Alliance

Finance

Bookkeeping Basics
What Every Nonprofit Bookkeeper Needs to Know
by Debra L. Ruegg and Lisa M. Venkatrathnam
Complete with step-by-step instructions, a glossary of accounting terms, detailed examples, and handy reproducible forms, this book will enable you to successfully meet the basic bookkeeping requirements of your nonprofit organization—even if you have little or no formal accounting training.
128 pages, softcover   Item # 069296

Coping with Cutbacks
The Nonprofit Guide to Success When Times Are Tight
by Emil Angelica and Vincent Hyman
Shows you practical ways to involve business, government, and other nonprofits to solve problems together. Also includes 185 cutback strategies you can put to use right away.
128 pages, softcover   Item # 069091

Financial Leadership for Nonprofit Executives
Guiding Your Organization to Long-term Success
by Jeanne Peters and Elizabeth Schaffer
Provides executives with a practical guide to protecting and growing the assets of their organizations and with accomplishing as much mission as possible with those resources.
144 pages, softcover   Item # 06944X

Venture Forth!
The Essential Guide to Starting a Moneymaking Business in Your Nonprofit Organization
by Rolfe Larson
The most complete guide on nonprofit business development. Building on the experience of dozens of organizations, this handbook gives you a time-tested approach for finding, testing, and launching a successful nonprofit business venture.
272 pages, softcover   Item # 069245

Marketing

The Fieldstone Alliance Nonprofit Guide to Conducting Successful Focus Groups
by Judith Sharken Simon
Shows how to collect valuable information without a lot of money or special expertise. Using this proven technique, you'll get essential opinions and feedback to help you check out your assumptions, do better strategic planning, improve services or products, and more.
80 pages, softcover   Item # 069199

Marketing Workbook for Nonprofit Organizations Volume I: Develop the Plan
by Gary J. Stern
Don't just wish for results—get them! Here's how to create a straightforward, usable marketing plan. Includes the six Ps of Marketing, how to use them effectively, a sample marketing plan, tips on using the Internet, and worksheets.
208 pages, softcover   Item # 069253

Marketing Workbook for Nonprofit Organizations Volume II: Mobilize People for Marketing Success
by Gary J. Stern
Put together a successful promotional campaign based on the most persuasive tool of all: personal contact. Learn how to mobilize your entire organization, its staff, volunteers, and supporters in a focused, one-to-one marketing campaign. Comes with *Pocket Guide for Marketing Representatives*. In it, your marketing representatives can record key campaign messages and find motivational reminders.
192 pages, softcover   Item # 069105

Message Matters
Succeeding at the Crossroads of Mission and Market
by Rebecca Leet
Today being heard demands delivering information that resonates with your audience's desires quickly, clearly, and continually. Message Matters gives you a simple framework for developing and using strategic messages so you can connect more successfully with your target audiences and compel them to action.
160 pages, softcover   Item # 069636

Management & Planning

The Accidental Techie
Supporting, Managing, and Maximizing Your Nonprofit's Technology
by Sue Bennett
How to support and manage technology on a day-to-day basis including: setting up a help desk, developing an effective technology budget and implementation plan, working with consultants and management, handling viruses, creating a backup system and schedule, purchasing hardware and software, and more.
176 pages, softcover   Item # 069490

Benchmarking for Nonprofits
How to Measure, Manage, and Improve Results
by Jason Saul
This book defines a formal, systematic, and reliable way to benchmark (the onging process of measuring your organization against leaders), from preparing your organization to measuring performance and implementing best practices.
128 pages, softcover   Item # 069431

For current prices, a catalog, or to order call ☎ 800-274-6024

Consulting with Nonprofits
A Practitioner's Guide
by Carol A. Lukas

A step-by-step, comprehensive guide for consultants. Addresses the art of consulting, how to run your business, and much more. Also includes tips and anecdotes from thirty skilled consultants.

240 pages, softcover   Item # 069172

The Fieldstone Alliance Nonprofit Guide to Crafting Effective Mission and Vision Statements
by Emil Angelica

Guides you through two six-step processes that result in a mission statement, vision statement, or both. Shows how a clarified mission and vision lead to more effective leadership, decisions, fundraising, and management. Includes tips, sample statements, and worksheets.

88 pages, softcover   Item # 06927X

The Fieldstone Alliance Nonprofit Guide to Developing Effective Teams
by Beth Gilbertsen and Vijit Ramchandani

Helps you understand, start, and maintain a team. Provides tools and techniques for writing a mission statement, setting goals, conducting effective meetings, creating ground rules to manage team dynamics, making decisions in teams, creating project plans, and developing team spirit.

80 pages, softcover   Item # 069202

The Five Life Stages of Nonprofit Organizations
Where You Are, Where You're Going, and What to Expect When You Get There
by Judith Sharken Simon with J. Terence Donovan

Shows you what's "normal" for each development stage which helps you plan for transitions, stay on track, and avoid unnecessary struggles. This guide also includes The Wilder Nonprofit Life Stage Assessment to plot and understand your organization's progress in seven arenas of organization development.

128 pages, softcover   Item # 069229

Generations
The Challenge of a Lifetime for Your Nonprofit
by Peter Brinckerhoff

What happens when a management team of all Baby Boomers leaves within a five year stretch? The clock is ticking....is your nonprofit ready? In this book, nonprofit mission expert Peter Brinckerhoff tells you what generational changes to expect and how to plan for them. You'll find in-depth information for each area of your organization—staff, board, volunteers, clients, marketing, technology, and finances.

232 pages, softcover   Item # 069555

Information Gold Mine
Innovative Uses of Evaluation
by Paul W. Mattessich, Shelly Hendricks, Ross VeLure Roholt

Don't underestimate the power of your evaluation findings. The real-life stories in this book clearly show the power of using evaluation data to produce good things for your nonprofit.

128 pages, softcover   Item # 069512

The Manager's Guide to Program Evaluation:
Planning, Contracting, and Managing for Useful Results
by Paul W. Mattessich, PhD

Explains how to plan and manage an evaluation that will help identify your organization's successes, share information with key audiences, and improve services.

96 pages, softcover   Item # 069385

The Nonprofit Mergers Workbook
The Leader's Guide to Considering, Negotiating, and Executing a Merger
by David La Piana

A merger can be a daunting and complex process. Save time, money, and untold frustration with this highly practical guide that makes the process manageable and controllable. Includes case studies, decision trees, twenty-two worksheets, checklists, tips, and complete step-by-step guidance from seeking partners to writing the merger agreement, and more.

240 pages, softcover   Item # 069210

The Nonprofit Mergers Workbook Part II
Unifying the Organization after a Merger
by La Piana Associates

Once the merger agreement is signed, the question becomes: How do we make this merger work? *Part II* helps you create a comprehensive plan to achieve *integration*—bringing together people, programs, processes, and systems from two (or more) organizations into a single, unified whole.

248 pages, includes CD-ROM   Item # 069415

Nonprofit Stewardship
A Better Way to Lead Your Mission-Based Organization
by Peter C. Brinckerhoff

You may lead a not-for-profit organization, but it's not your organization. It belongs to the community it serves. You are the steward—the manager of resources that belong to someone else. The stewardship model of leadership can help your organization improve its mission capability by forcing you to keep your organization's mission foremost. It helps you make decisions that are best for the people your organization serves. In other words, stewardship helps you do more good for more people.

272 pages, softcover   Item # 069423

For current prices or to order visit us online at 🖥 www.fieldstonealliance.org

Resolving Conflict in Nonprofit Organizations
The Leader's Guide to Finding Constructive Solutions
by Marion Peters Angelica

Helps you identify conflict, decide whether to intervene, uncover and deal with the true issues, and design and conduct a conflict resolution process. Includes exercises to learn and practice conflict resolution skills, guidance on handling unique conflicts such as harassment and discrimination, and when (and where) to seek outside help with litigation, arbitration, and mediation.

192 pages, softcover   Item # 069164

Strategic Planning Workbook for Nonprofit Organizations, Revised and Updated
by Bryan Barry

Chart a wise course for your nonprofit's future. This time-tested workbook gives you practical step-by-step guidance, real-life examples, one nonprofit's complete strategic plan, and easy-to-use worksheets.

120 pages, softcover   Item # 069075
Includes CD-ROM with worksheets and templates

Community Building

Community Building: What Makes It Work
by Wilder Research Center

Reveals twenty-eight keys to help you build community more effectively. Includes detailed descriptions of each factor, case examples of how they play out, and practical questions to assess your work.

112 pages, softcover   Item # 069121

Community Economic Development Handbook
by Mihailo Temali

A concrete, practical handbook to turning any neighborhood around. It explains how to start a community economic development organization, and then lays out the steps of four proven and powerful strategies for revitalizing inner-city neighborhoods.

288 pages, softcover   Item # 069369

Community Leadership Handbook
by James F. Krile with Gordon Curphy and Duane R. Lund

Leadership is a choice, not a position. You can improve your community, and this hands-on guide shows you how. Based on the best of Blandin Foundation's 20-year experience in developing community leaders, it gives community members—like yourself—the tools to bring people together to make changes.

216 pages, softcover   Item # 069547

The Fieldstone Alliance Nonprofit Guide to Conducting Community Forums
by Carol Lukas and Linda Hoskins

Provides step-by-step instruction to plan and carry out exciting, successful community forums that will educate the public, build consensus, focus action, or influence policy.

128 pages, softcover   Item # 069318

The Creative Community Builder's Handbook
by Tom Borrup

Art and culture can be a powerful catalyst for revitalizing the economic, social, and physical conditions in communities. This handbook gives you successful strategies, best practices, and "how-to" guidance to turn cultural gems into effective community change.

280 pages, softcover   Item # 069474

Crossing Borders, Sharing Journeys
Effective Capacity Building with Immigrant and Refugee Groups
by Sarah Gleason

This report outlines seven broad factors found to contribute to effective capacity building with immigrant and refugee lead organizations (IRLOs). Case studies illustrate practices used when working with IRLOs and highlights principles that other capacity builders can apply when working with similar groups. You can also download a free copy of this report at www.FieldstoneAlliance.org.

88 pages, softcover   Item # 069628

New Americans, New Promise
A Guide to the Refugee Journey in America
by Yorn Yan

Gain a better understanding of the refugee experience in the U.S. Refugee-serving organizations will find solid, practical advice for how to best help refugees through the acculturation and transition process of becoming a New American. Refugees will discover what to expect during five stages of development that they typically progress through as they adapt to their new home.

200 pages, softcover   Item # 069504

Collaboration

Collaboration Handbook
Creating, Sustaining, and Enjoying the Journey
by Michael Winer and Karen Ray

Shows you how to get a collaboration going, set goals, determine everyone's roles, create an action plan, and evaluate the results. Includes a case study of one collaboration from start to finish, helpful tips on how to avoid pitfalls, and worksheets to keep everyone on track.

192 pages, softcover   Item # 069032

The Fieldstone Alliance Nonprofit Guide to Forming Alliances
Working Together to Achieve Mutual Goals
by Linda Hoskins, Emil Angelica

Alliances make good sense for nonprofits, much of the time. But success with alliances requires that they be used wisely, and with a good understanding of which kinds of alliances will result in the best outcomes given the conditions and need. This guide will help you understand and strategically form alliances that work at a lower level of intensity.

112 pages, softcover   Item # 069466

For current prices, a catalog, or to order call 800-274-6024

The Nimble Collaboration
Fine-Tuning Your Collaboration for Lasting Success
by Karen Ray

Shows you ways to make your existing collaboration more responsive, flexible, and productive. Provides three key strategies to help your collaboration respond quickly to changing environments and participants.

136 pages, softcover   Item # 069288

Lobbying & Advocacy

The Lobbying and Advocacy Handbook for Nonprofit Organizations
Shaping Public Policy at the State and Local Level
by Marcia Avner

The Lobbying and Advocacy Handbook is a planning guide and resource for nonprofit organizations that want to influence issues that matter to them. This book will help you decide whether to lobby and then put plans in place to make it work.

240 pages, softcover   Item # 069261

The Nonprofit Board Member's Guide to Lobbying and Advocacy
by Marcia Avner

Written specifically for board members, this guide helps organizations increase their impact on policy decisions. It reveals how board members can be involved in planning for and implementing successful lobbying efforts.

96 pages, softcover   Item # 069393

Board Tools

The Best of the Board Café
Hands-on Solutions for Nonprofit Boards
by Jan Masaoka, CompassPoint Nonprofit Services

Gathers the most requested articles from the e-newsletter, *Board Café*. You'll find a lively menu of ideas, information, opinions, news, and resources to help board members give and get the most out of their board service.

232 pages, softcover   Item # 069407

The Nonprofit Board Member's Guide to Lobbying and Advocacy
by Marcia Avner

Board members are uniquely positioned to be effective and influential lobbyists. This guide spells out how your board can use their power and privilege to move your nonprofit's work forward.

96 pages, softcover   Item # 069393

Keeping the Peace
Resolving Conflict in the Boardroom
by Marion Angelica

Written especially for board members and chief executives, this book is a step-by-step guide to ensure that everyone is treated fairly and a feasible solution is reached.

48 pages, softcover   Item # 860127

Funder's Guides

Community Visions, Community Solutions
Grantmaking for Comprehensive Impact
by Joseph A. Connor and Stephanie Kadel-Taras

Helps foundations, community funds, government agencies, and other grantmakers uncover a community's highest aspiration for itself, and support and sustain strategic efforts to get to workable solutions.

128 pages, softcover   Item # 06930X

A Funder's Guide to Evaluation
Leveraging Evaluation to Improve Nonprofit Effectiveness
by Peter York

More and more funders and nonprofit leaders are shifting away from proving something to someone else, and toward *im*-proving what they do so they can achieve their mission and share how they succeeded with others. This book includes strategies and tools to help grantmakers support and use evaluation as a nonprofit organizational capacity-building tool.

160 pages, softcover   Item # 069482

A Funder's Guide to Organizational Assessment
Tools, Processes, and Their Use in Building Capacity
Editor: Lori Bartczak

Funders, grantees, and consultants will understand how organizational assessment can be used to 1) Build the capacity of nonprofits, 2) Enhance grantmaking, 3) Impact organizational systems, 4) Strengthen the nonprofit sector, and 5) Measure foundation effectiveness. The guide presents four grantee assessment tools and two tools for assessing foundation performance.

216 pages, softcover   Item # 069539

Power in Policy
A Funder's Guide to Advocacy and Civic Participation
Editor: David F. Arons

Increasingly, foundations are finding that participation in public decision making is often a critical component in reaching the impact demanded by mission-related goals. For those weighing precisely what role foundations should play, the mix of real-life examples, practical advice, and inspiration in this book are invaluable.

320 pages, softcover   Item # 069458

Strengthening Nonprofit Performance
A Funder's Guide to Capacity Building
by Paul Connolly and Carol Lukas

This practical guide synthesizes the most recent capacity building practice and research into a collection of strategies, steps, and examples that you can use to get started on or improve funding to strengthen nonprofit organizations.

176 pages, softcover   Item # 069377

For current prices or to order visit us online at www.fieldstonealliance.org